At Issue

Should Drilling Be Permitted in the Arctic National Wildlife Refuge?

Other Books in the At Issue Series:

At Issue

Should Drilling Be Permitted in the Arctic National Wildlife Refuge?

David M. Haugen, Book Editor

GREENHAVEN PRESS
A part of Gale, Cengage Learning

GALE
CENGAGE Learning

Detroit • New York • San Francisco • New Haven, Conn • Waterville, Maine • London

GALE
CENGAGE Learning·

Christine Nasso, *Publisher*
Elizabeth Des Chenes, *Managing Editor*

© 2008 Greenhaven Press, a part of Gale, Cengage Learning.

Gale and Greenhaven Press are registered trademarks used herein under license.

For more information, contact:
Greenhaven Press
27500 Drake Rd.
Farmington Hills, MI 48331-3535
Or you can visit our Internet site at gale.cengage.com

For product information and technology assistance, contact us at

Gale Customer Support, 1-800-877-4253
For permission to use material from this text or product, submit all requests online at www.cengage.com/permissions

Further permissions questions can be emailed to permissionrequest@cengage.com

Articles in Greenhaven Press anthologies are often edited for length to meet page requirements. In addition, original titles of these works are changed to clearly present the main thesis and to explicitly indicate the author's opinion. Every effort is made to ensure that Greenhaven Press accurately reflects the original intent of the authors. Every effort has been made to trace the owners of copyrighted material.

Cover photograph reproduced by permission of Debra Hughes 2007. Used under license from Shutterstock.com.

LIBRARY OF CONGRESS CATALOGING-IN-PUBLICATION DATA

Should drilling be permitted in the Arctic National Wildlife Refuge? / David M. Haugen, book editor.
    p. cm. -- (At issue)
  Includes bibliographical references and index.
  ISBN-13: 978-0-7377-3930-5 (hardcover)
  ISBN-13: 978-0-7377-3931-2 (pbk.)
  1. Oil well drilling--Environmental aspects--Alaska--Arctic National Wildlife Refuge.
  2. Arctic National Wildlife Refuge (Alaska). I. Haugen, David M., 1969-
  QP279.S56 2008
  333.95'416097987--dc22
                                                                    2007051383

Printed in the United States of America
3 4 5 6 7 12 11 10 09

Contents

Introduction

Originally mandated by a public order in 1960, the Arctic National Wildlife Refuge (ANWR) is a federally protected region of northeastern Alaska set aside "for the purpose of preserving unique wildlife, wilderness and recreational values." When it was established by President Dwight D. Eisenhower, the ANWR was less than 10 million acres in size, but President Jimmy Carter subsequently expanded it in 1980 to its current size of more than 19 million acres (with 8 million acres of the original refuge designated as U.S. wilderness).

At the time of the ANWR's expansion, a strip of coastal plain along the Beaufort Sea was reserved for geologic study to determine if this 1.5-million-acre area might contain deposits of oil and other natural resources that could be developed. The 1002 Area—as the strip of land is called—was surveyed in 1988 and again ten years later. The initial assessment concluded that little recoverable oil was available in the region, but the 1998 survey countered that opinion and suggested that significant reserves of crude oil lie beneath the plain. These findings have made the relatively small piece of coastal territory the centerpiece of political controversy ever since.

Citing the 1998 survey, the United States Energy Information Administration (EIA) estimates that around 10 billion barrels of recoverable oil may be locked up under the refuge. The EIA also projects that it would take between seven and twelve years from the initial approval stage to begin full-scale production. Given the steadily rising prices of imported oil and the pronouncements that the world has reached its peak of oil production, it is understandable why proponents of developing the 1002 region have insisted that delays are costly. In testimony before a House of Representatives committee in 2003, secretary of the interior Gale Norton pushed to open up the region by arguing, "Our reliance on foreign oil has impacts on the lives of American families, farmers and workers—as the current gasoline price increase shows. As long as we have planes, trains and automobiles powered by oil and gas, we will need a homegrown, stable, reliable source of supply." Norton also suggested that drilling in the refuge would mean more jobs for Americans and would provide revenue for the government, which would in part fund research into alternative energies to ease foreign oil dependence.

Other proponents claim that opening the 1002 Area to development would not entail destroying the ecological or recreational value of the refuge. Arctic Power, a grassroots collective of Alaskans in favor of oil exploration in the ANWR, maintains that improvements in drilling techniques have reduced the "footprint" of extraction equipment in recent decades. Comparing modern methods with those used to drill in other parts of Alaska in the 1970s, Arctic Power states: "New directional drilling techniques and drill equipment allow wells to be spaced 25 to 15 feet apart, and in some cases 10 feet apart. A drill pad that would have been 65 acres in 1977 can be less than nine acres today. The same number of wells that required a 65-acre pad in the 1970's can be drilled on less than a nine-acre pad today." The organization also insists that the use of ice pads and ice access roads—instead of their gravel or cement counterparts—to reach drilling sites will allow all traces of drilling to disappear after a site has been completely tapped.

Environmentalists are not persuaded by these images of eco-friendly drilling. Quoted in a 2005 *Economist* article, Pamela A. Miller, a former employee of the U.S. Fish and Wildlife Service, states that that rosy picture does not match reality because not all oil companies feel the need to use the most environmentally responsible—which are also the most expensive—drilling methods, especially in an isolated region where few people live or visit. But according to her, the technology arguments are immaterial; as she contends, "It is a land use issue that involves changing the dominant purpose of an area set aside for that reason from a wilderness to an oilfield."

Most opponents of developing the wildlife refuge claim that they favor keeping the land in its natural state to protect the migratory animals that traverse the barren landscape. A chief concern is the Porcupine River caribou herd, which moves back and forth across the ANWR and parts of northern Canada. This herd uses the coastal plain in the 1002 Area as a calving ground in the late spring, and preservationists fear that drilling in the region will interfere with birthrates. They argue that a decrease in calving would have repercussions for both the herd and the native Gwich'in people in the area who rely on caribou for food and other resources. As the Gwich'in Steering Committee, a communal voice for the native villages, attests, "Drilling in the Arctic Refuge would violate the human rights of the Gwich'in people because of the impacts drilling would have on Gwich'in subsistence, culture, and way of life."

Others who wish to keep the ANWR pristine assert that those who claim that vast reserves of oil exist under the coastal plain are purposely masking the real issue—namely that more drilling will not solve the nation's energy crisis. These defenders of the ANWR claim that America has to focus on implementing energy conservation, creating fuel-efficient vehicles, and researching alternative energies instead of simply protracting the country's dependence on what everyone agrees is a limited resource. "Reducing oil consumption and increasing Corporate Average Fuel Economy—or CAFE—standards is the better route to energy security," insisted Senator Dianne Feinstein of California in a 2003 statement for the *Congressional Record* regarding opening the ANWR.

Feinstein, like all her colleagues on Capitol Hill, has been part of the ongoing congressional debate over drilling in the 1002 Area since the 1990s. Proposals to open the region have been tucked into several energy bills that have always passed either the House of Representatives or the Senate only to be stymied in the other house. In early 2007 House Democrats took a different tack and proposed legislation to permanently close the entire wildlife refuge to oil exploration. No action has yet been taken on this bill. The congressional stalemate on this debate, however, indicates how strongly held the views are on both sides. In *At Issue: Should Drilling Be Permitted in the Arctic National Wildlife Refuge?* several proponents and opponents lay out the fundamentals of this national controversy and explore the consequences of tapping or ignoring the region's potential oil supply.

1

Drilling in the ANWR Will Reduce America's Dependence on Foreign Oil

Jerome Corsi

Jerome Corsi is a staff reporter for the conservative online news-paper World Net Daily. *He holds a PhD in political science from Harvard University and has authored numerous books concerning American government and foreign policy, particularly on issues regarding the Middle East and oil.*

The United States imports around 60 percent of the oil that it uses every year. In order to keep trade relations open and friendly, the U.S. government must remain uncritical of the governments and policies of oil exporting countries and must often intervene in areas where America's oil interests are threatened. Drilling for oil in the Arctic National Wildlife Reserve would allow the United States to produce more domestic oil, thus reducing its foreign oil dependency and helping preserve national security.

The Congressional Office of Technology and Assessment reports that oil exploration in the Alaska National Wildlife Reserve [ANWR] . . . would require only about 5,000 to 7,000 acres, one-half of 1 percent of ANWR, or about 0.004 percent (four one-thousands percent) of Alaska's total land mass. Putting together Prudhoe Bay [the location of an existing oil field development in the North Slope Borough of

Alaska] with the coastal area of ANWR that may be opened to oil exploration and you still get an area that is about the size of a postage stamp on a football field. Prudhoe Bay's gravel pads, gathering lines, production facilities, roads and other infrastructures occupy less than 6,000 acres of land, yet Prudhoe Bay remains America's largest oil field.

The Energy Information Agency of the Department of Energy estimates that Alaska oil production averaged 902,000 barrels of oil per day from January through August 2004, about 16 percent of total U.S. oil production during that period, most of which comes from Prudhoe Bay. Opening up even a limited area of ANWR for drilling would offer the prospect of producing from Alaska possibly 40 percent or more of the oil consumed in America.

Today we have to have foreign entanglements because we have to import foreign oil.

The Source of U.S. Foreign Policy Problems

In writing "Black Gold Stranglehold: The Myth of Scarcity and the Politics of Oil," Craig Smith and I calculated the cost of importing foreign oil:

> Each day we import some 12 million barrels of oil, about 60 percent of all the oil we consume. About 20 percent of our oil imports come from Persian Gulf countries, averaging about 2.4 million barrels a day. At $50 a barrel, this means we are sending more than $600 million a day overseas for oil, of which $120 million a day goes to Persian Gulf countries.

> At $60 a barrel, we are sending $720 million a day overseas for oil, of which $144 million goes to the Persian Gulf. With oil at $60 a barrel, we are sending overseas nearly a quarter of a trillion dollars each year just to buy oil.

We have never before in our history experienced this massive a transfer of our wealth overseas. Moreover, our dependence upon foreign countries means we are increasingly vulnerable to being held hostage [for] oil. Do we not send back the flood of Mexican illegal immigrants crossing our borders because we import 1.75 million barrels of oil a day from Mexico? Are we forced to tolerate [president of Venezuela] Hugo Chavez's socialism and insults to America because we import 1.3 million barrels of oil a day?

The internal politics of our foreign oil partners can directly affect us by their willingness to open up or shut down the oil spigot. Today we have to have foreign entanglements because we have to import foreign oil.

Environmental Extremists' Actions Benefit Foreign Interests

Perhaps the Sierra Club [environmental organization] ought to be forced to register as a foreign lobbyist for Saudi Aramco [the national oil company of Saudi Arabia]? Certainly foreign oil companies have no better friend in America than radical extremists who stand in the way of every effort to produce more oil in Alaska and offshore, where we know we have oil not currently registered in our foreign reserves. Why not? Radical environmentalists will not tolerate any new exploration of oil in America, no matter how reasonable or environmentally responsible.

Listening to the environmentalists, we could almost get the impression that they don't want even limited exploration of ANWR because they are afraid of how much oil we might find in Alaska. How many working motorists forced to pay $50 to $75 to fill their gas tanks can still afford their Sierra Club memberships? When we move to 70 percent dependence on foreign oil, will working Americans still be comfortable to leave billions of barrels of unexplored oil in the ground under Alaska and offshore?

These are important questions, especially when the Senate has raised the question of confiscating oil company "windfall profits." We have argued that the oil companies need to realize they have obligations to be socially responsible. What is the oil company plan to invest profits in refineries? We have not built a new refinery in the United States in the last 30 years. This is a key part of the "stranglehold." Even if we drilled more oil in ANWR, we could not get more gasoline into the pump unless we expand our refining capabilities.

Finding a Balance

We call here for more hearings, this time with the environmentalists. Let's get a balance between protecting every caribou and allowing some reasonable exploration of domestic oil so we can take an important step away from foreign oil dependence. Let's arrive at a reasonable formula for the environmental barriers to building new refineries so we can press oil company executives to put more capital into the supply side of the equation.

By removing the ANWR drilling provisions from the House budget bill [in 2005], GOP congressmen who want to move to the center by appearing more "green" have probably achieved this limited objective. But are these same congressmen willing to face constituents when the voting public realizes each concession to radical environmentalism is another move away from increasing domestic supplies we badly need—not only to keep oil prices affordable, but to make sure we do not compromise our national security on the altar of keeping all environments "pristine"?

2

Drilling in the ANWR Will Not Reduce America's Dependence on Foreign Oil

Natural Resources Defense Council

The Natural Resources Defense Council (NRDC), founded in 1970, is a nonprofit membership organization that advocates for the preservation of the environment worldwide. NRDC has consistently opposed opening the Arctic National Wildlife Refuge for oil exploration and production.

The Arctic National Wildlife Refuge (ANWR), designated a wildlife reserve in 1960, ranks among other national natural treasures such as Yellowstone National Park and the Grand Canyon and should be protected accordingly. Drilling for oil in the refuge would destroy the pristine setting of this wilderness. More significantly, the limited supply of oil taken from ANWR would not provide the United States any lasting energy security or reduce our dependence on oil from foreign countries. Instead, the government should be investigating alternative energies and developing more fuel-efficient technologies to achieve energy independence.

On the northern edge of our continent, stretching from the peaks of the Brooks Range across a vast expanse of tundra to the Beaufort Sea, lies Alaska's Arctic National Wildlife Refuge. An American Serengeti [an African plain teeming with wildlife], the Arctic Refuge continues to pulse with million-year-old ecological rhythms. It is the greatest living reminder that conserving nature in its wild state is a core American value.

In 2005, Congress twice affirmed their constituents' belief that America's remaining wilds are important and rejection of claims that Arctic Refuge oil is any sort of answer to the nation's dependence on foreign oil. In November 2005, leaders of the House removed provisions that would have allowed drilling in the refuge from a massive budget bill. And in December 2005, the Senate withstood an attempt by Republican leaders to attach Arctic drilling to a "must-pass" defense spending bill.

Despite these stinging defeats to their agenda, President [George W.] Bush and pro-drilling forces in Congress are as intent as ever on opening the refuge to oil and gas interests. . . .

The truth is, we simply can't drill our way to energy independence.

The Danger of a Corporate Takeover

The controversy over drilling in the Arctic Refuge—the last piece of America's Arctic coastline not already open to oil exploration—isn't new. Big Oil has long sought access to the refuge's coastal plain, a fragile swath of tundra that teems with staggering numbers of birds and animals. During the Bush administration's first term, repeated attempts were made to open the refuge. But time after time, the American public rejected the idea. Congress has received hundreds of thousands of emails, faxes and phone calls from citizens opposed to drilling in the Arctic Refuge, an outpouring that has helped make the difference. And polls have consistently shown that a solid majority of Americans oppose drilling; a December 2004 Zogby Survey found that 55 percent of respondents oppose drilling, and that 59 percent consider attaching this issue to the budget process to be a "backdoor maneuver."

Despite repeated failure and stiff opposition, drilling proponents press on. Why? They believe that opening the Arctic Refuge will turn the corner in the broader national debate over whether or not energy, timber, mining and other industries should be allowed into pristine wild areas across the country. Next up: Greater Yellowstone? Our Western canyonlands? Our coastal waters?

The drive to drill the Arctic Refuge is about oil company profits and lifting barriers to future exploration in protected lands, pure and simple. It has nothing to do with energy independence. Opening the Arctic Refuge to energy development is about transferring our public estate into corporate hands, so it can be liquidated for a quick buck.

An Inadequate Solution

What would America gain by allowing heavy industry into the refuge? Very little. Oil from the refuge would hardly make a dent in our dependence on foreign imports—leaving our economy and way of life just as exposed to wild swings in worldwide oil prices and supply as it is today. The truth is, we simply can't drill our way to energy independence.

Although drilling proponents often say there are 16 billion barrels of oil under the refuge's coastal plain, the U.S. Geological [Survey]'s estimate of the amount that could be recovered economically—that is, the amount likely to be profitably extracted and sold—represents less than a year's U.S. supply.

It would take 10 years for any Arctic Refuge oil to reach the market, and even when production peaks—in the distant year of 2027—the refuge would produce a paltry 1 or 2 percent of Americans' daily consumption. Whatever oil the refuge might produce is simply irrelevant to the larger issue of meeting America's future energy needs.

The Cost Is Too High

Oil produced from the Arctic Refuge would come at enormous, and irreversible, cost. The refuge is among the world's last true wildernesses, and it is one of the largest sanctuaries for Arctic animals. Traversed by a dozen rivers and framed by jagged peaks, this spectacular wilderness is a vital birthing ground for polar bears, grizzlies, Arctic wolves, caribou and the endangered shaggy musk ox, a mammoth-like survivor of the last Ice Age.

For a sense of what big oil's heavy machinery would do to the refuge, just look 60 miles west to Prudhoe Bay—a gargantuan oil complex that has turned 1,000 square miles of fragile tundra into a sprawling industrial zone containing 1,500 miles of roads and pipelines, 1,400 producing wells and three jetports. The result is a landscape defaced by mountains of sewage sludge, scrap metal, garbage and more than 60 contaminated waste sites that contain—and often leak—acids, lead, pesticides, solvents and diesel fuel.

The solution to America's energy problems will be found in American ingenuity, not more oil.

While proponents of drilling insist the Arctic Refuge could be developed by disturbing as little as 2,000 acres within the 1.5-million-acre coastal plain, a recent analysis by NRDC reveals this to be pure myth. Why? Because U.S. Geological Survey studies have found that oil in the refuge isn't concentrated in a single, large reservoir. Rather, it's spread across the coastal plain in more than 30 small deposits, which would require vast networks of roads and pipelines that would fragment the habitat, disturbing and displacing wildlife.

The Promise of American Innovation

The solution to America's energy problems will be found in American ingenuity, not more oil. Only by reducing our reliance on oil—foreign and domestic—and investing in cleaner, renewable forms of power will our country achieve true energy security. The good news is that we already have many of the tools we need to accomplish this. For example, Detroit has the technology right now to produce high-performance hybrid cars, trucks and SUVs; if America made the transition to these more efficient vehicles, far more oil would be saved than the Arctic Refuge is likely to produce. Doesn't that make far more sense than selling out our natural heritage and exploiting one of our true wilderness gems?

3

Drilling in the ANWR Would Likely Endanger Caribou Herds

Kenneth R. Whitten

Kenneth R. Whitten is a retired research biologist for the Alaska Department of Fish and Game.

The largest oil development in the United States, the Prudhoe Bay oil field, has had a negative impact on the growth of the central Arctic caribou herd that uses this land for its calving grounds. It is likely that the effects of human and industrial presence on this herd, such as the herd's avoidance of highly trafficked areas and relocation to new calving grounds, would be mirrored by the Porcupine River caribou herd if development were to take place in its home in the Arctic National Wildlife Refuge (ANWR). The Porcupine herd is more concentrated than the central Arctic herd and has slower reproductive rates, suggesting that interference in its primary calving grounds in the ANWR would be even more detrimental to its survivability as a herd.

Each caribou herd has its own, discrete calving area. Other seasonal habitats for caribou tend to be widespread, but the combined features of scarce predators and high quality forage that characterize calving areas usually occur together on only a small portion of a herd's overall range. Therefore calving grounds are considered to be critical habitats. Prudhoe

Kenneth R. Whitten, "Caribou and Oil Development on the North Slope," *Testimony to the U.S. House Resources Committee at Hearing on Republican Energy Bill, "Energy Security Act,"* July 11, 2001. Reproduced by permission of the author.

Bay and other operating oilfields on the North Slope are within the calving grounds of the Central Arctic Herd. This herd was quite small (only about 5,000) when oil development first started in the mid-1970s, but impacts from development were soon noted. Calving within the Prudhoe Field had already largely ceased by the time oil first began flowing south. The dense network of pipelines, roads, oil wells, and production facilities at Prudhoe Bay also blocked mid-summer movements of caribou along the arctic coast. Cow and calf caribou avoided the Trans Alaska Pipeline Corridor but continued to cross it successfully from late summer through spring, when calves were older and the herd was south of the intensely developed oilfields.

Oil Development Effects on Caribou

In spite of these impacts, the Central Arctic Herd thrived during the early years of oil development and grew to about 14,000 by 1983. By the time development expanded into the Kuparuk area during the 1980s, the petroleum industry had begun to consolidate facilities so that the newer oilfields disturbed less space. Also, some pipelines were raised higher above ground and separated from roads with heavy traffic. These new designs allowed caribou to move more freely than at Prudhoe Bay, and caribou continued to use the Kuparuk and Milne Pt. Oilfields. Nevertheless, caribou with newborn calves avoided developed areas, even when there was little traffic. Over time, the Kuparuk and Milne Fields became more heavily developed, and caribou used them less and less.

By the late 1980s, growth of the Central Arctic Herd slowed, and the population stabilized at about 23,000. Harsh climatic conditions, including severe winters and dry summer growing seasons, stressed caribou throughout much of Alaska during the early 1990s. Central Arctic caribou that spent more time in or near the oilfields gained less weight during the summer growing season and had lower pregnancy rates and lower calf survival that other members of the herd that seldom encountered development. Avoidance of roads and pipelines during calving was thought to be causing abandonment of preferred habitats and overuse [of] undisturbed habitats. Chronic disruption of summer movements also exacerbated exposure of caribou to insect pests. The Central Arctic Herd declined to 18,000 in 1993 and then grew slowly to about 20,000 in 1995.

By the late 1990s, the ever expanding oilfields were displacing even more caribou during calving. Forage quality on newly occupied calving grounds south and west of the oilfields was lower than in the former oilfield calving area. Nevertheless, favorable weather once again prevailed in the range of the Central Arctic Herd. Calf productivity and survival recovered and the Central Arctic Herd once again increased rapidly, reaching 27,000 in the year 2000.

The Imminent Impact of Development

The United States Congress continues to debate expansion of North Slope oil development onto the coastal plain of the Arctic National Wildlife Refuge. The potential lease area within the Arctic Refuge lies within the calving grounds of the Porcupine Caribou Herd. This large, migratory herd moves between the U.S. and Canada and is vital to the traditional subsistence cultures of numerous Native villages in both countries. Over the past 25 years, the Porcupine Herd has fluctuated between about 100,000 and 180,000 animals, with the [2001] population [numbering] about 120,000.

Viability of the Porcupine Herd population depends on the high calf survival rates experienced on the Coastal Plain.

Porcupine Herd caribou are much more concentrated on their calving grounds than the smaller Central Arctic Herd. Although calving has occurred historically over a fairly large area of the North Slope in Alaska and the Yukon Territory, most calves are usually born in a smaller region that encompasses most of the area being considered for oil development. During late June and early July, essentially all cows and calves and many bulls of the Porcupine Herd use the potential development area every year.

Even during periods of relatively mild climatic conditions, Porcupine Herd caribou have tended to have somewhat lower calf production and adult survival rates than most other caribou herds. In contrast, calf survival in the Porcupine Herd has generally been very high when females have been able to calve on the traditional calving area that includes the potential oil lease area. As with other caribou calving areas, rapid, nutritious plant growth often occurs in this area during calving, and the coastal plain is also relatively free of predators. Calf survival has been lower when late snowmelt forced Porcupine Herd caribou to calve in nearby mountains and foothills where wolves, grizzly bears, and golden eagles abound. Viability of the Porcupine Herd population depends on the high calf survival rates experienced on the Coastal Plain.

The Porcupine Herd could experience adverse population level impacts from development.

Studies in the Prudhoe Bay and Kuparuk oilfields show that larger groups (100 or more caribou) have difficulty crossing roads and pipes. Porcupine Herd caribou normally occur in much larger groups than Central Arctic Herd caribou. Groups of several thousand caribou occur throughout the summer in the Porcupine Herd, and from mid-June through July group sizes in the tens of thousands are common.

Ties Between Humans and Caribou

In summary, development of the Prudhoe Bay oilfield displaced caribou and disrupted their movements. Similar long-term displacement now appears to be occurring elsewhere, even in the "state-of-the-art" Kuparuk and Milne Pt. Oilfields. When climate has been generally favorable, the Central Arctic Herd has been able to hold its own and even increase, in spite of displacement from some of its favored habitats. In times of environmental stress, however, Central Arctic caribou that regularly used the oilfields fared poorly relative to other members of the herd that used areas away from development. The entire population then declined. Mitigation measures that appeared to work fairly well in the early stages of North Slope oilfield development may thus become less effective as more and more of the Central Arctic Herd's preferred habitats are developed and more caribou are concentrated on the habitats that remain accessible.

We cannot be certain that even current state-of-the-art mitigation measures will guarantee access to critical habitats for the larger, more densely aggregated Porcupine Herd. Environmental resources at risk in development [of] the Arctic National Wildlife Refuge are considerable. The Porcupine Herd far exceeds the Central Arctic Herd in importance as a regional subsistence resource. Preferred coastal plain habitats in the Arctic Refuge are much narrower (10–40 miles wide) than in the range of the Central Arctic Herd (100–150 miles wide). Disturbance has so far only displaced Central Arctic caribou to other coastal plain habitats with few predators. If similar spatial displacement were to occur in the Arctic Refuge, however, caribou would be driven to foothills and mountains with more abundant predators and/or lower quality forage. Consequently, the Porcupine Herd might not fare as well as the Central Arctic Herd apparently did during the early years of Prudhoe Bay development. The Porcupine Herd could experience adverse population level impacts from development even during periods of mild weather. Any impacts that would cause a long-term decline in calf survival could lower average population size over time, with serious consequences for many residents in both Canada and the U.S.

Considering the importance of the Porcupine Caribou Herd to indigenous people in the United States and Canada, and the high likelihood that petroleum leasing and development would cause long-term harm to those caribou, 21 arctic caribou biologists from the US and Canada signed a letter to former President [Bill] Clinton urging permanent protection of the Porcupine Herd calving grounds from development. Over 500 prominent North American scientists signed a letter to President [George W.] Bush urging protection of the Arctic Refuge Coastal Plain to safeguard caribou and other natural resource values. Protection of the Coastal Plain has also been endorsed by the Alaska Chapter of The Wildlife Society, the American Society of Mammalogists, and the Cooper Ornithological Union.

4

Drilling in the ANWR Would Be Compatible with Caribou Herds

Matthew A. Cronin

Matthew A. Cronin, a research associate professor, specializes in the study of animal population genetics and phylogenetics at the School of Natural Resources and Agricultural Sciences of the University of Alaska in Fairbanks. He is also currently the science advisor for Alaska's Office of the Governor.

Although drilling for oil has gone on for thirty years at the Prudhoe Bay oil field in Alaska, populations of wildlife in the area have grown or remained stable. In particular, the caribou herd in the region has experienced significant growth over this time despite sharing its calving lands with oil companies. Given that drilling technologies have improved since the 1970s, it is likely that the Porcupine River caribou herd would also suffer no great hardship if oil exploration began in its home range in the Arctic National Wildlife Refuge. Caribou are resourceful animals and can utilize new calving grounds if their territory is disturbed.

The Arctic National Wildlife Refuge (ANWR) in the northeast corner of Alaska, is considered the best onshore prospect in the United States for a major oil discovery. Yet, exploration for oil and gas has not occurred. Contested by environmental groups and government agency biologists because of environmental concerns, particularly about wildlife, the biased, negative appraisals of the impacts of oil fields on wildlife that these groups present serve to misinform both the public and elected officials.

To assess the potential environmental concerns about ANWR, it is instructive to review the experience in the existing Alaska oil fields at Prudhoe Bay. Antidevelopment advocates claim that the oil fields have had serious impacts on wildlife. The fact is that populations of caribou, grizzly bears, polar bears, arctic foxes, and musk oxen have all grown or remained stable over the 30-year period of oil exploration and development.

Statistics Showing Growth Are Often Ignored

A particularly important example is the central Arctic caribou herd that occurs in the Prudhoe Bay region. This herd has grown more than 500 percent since the oil fields were developed. Caribou in these areas frequently have had higher calf/cow ratios than in undeveloped areas, continue to calve in oil field areas, and use oil field habitats extensively during the summer. This includes frequent use of oil field roads and structures for travel and to escape from insects. These findings have been published in scientific journals, but they are frequently ignored or downplayed by government biologists and environmental groups. This has been most apparent in the last few years as government biologists publish documents continuing to claim significant impacts of the oil fields on caribou, despite the herd's steady growth.

The selective use of information by the antidevelopment groups is apparent in the recent National Research Council's (NRC) report, "Cumulative Environmental Effects of Oil and Gas Activities on Alaska's North Slope." During the caribou herd's overall growth from 5,000 animals in the 1970s to 32,000 in 2002, there was a decline between 1992 and 1995. It was most apparent in the western part of the herd's range that contains the oil fields. This was followed by an increase between 1995 and 2000. The NRC report incredibly ignored the overall herd increase, and attributed the 1992–1995 declines to the oil fields, combined with increased harassment by mosquitoes and flies.

In 2001, the U.S. Fish & Wildlife Service also attributed the decline to the oil fields, but this time it was in combination with bad winter weather. It would be obviously biased to say the oil fields only caused a decline in some years and ignore the overall growth of the herd. The biologists therefore came up with secondary impacts such as weather or insects to support their claims. The NRC report also ignored the fact that a neighboring herd, without oil field development in its range, had the same trend of increase, then a slight decrease in the mid-1990s, followed by another increase. This suggests that environmental factors, not oil fields, determine the herd's numbers.

Caribou continue to calve in areas with oil fields, and avoidance of the roads and facilities is limited to a few weeks around the calving period.

In papers published in *The Journal of Wildlife Research* and *The Wildlife Society Bulletin*, my co-authors and I suggested that the decline in caribou numbers between 1992 and 1995 was likely due to movements between oil field ranges and undeveloped ranges, and not to impacts from the oil fields. As numbers in the developed (oil field) areas went down, numbers in the undeveloped areas went up by about the same amount. Clearly, movement of the highly mobile caribou between areas is a reasonable interpretation. However, these papers were ignored in the NRC report.

Perhaps the most important point regarding Prudhoe Bay is that the management objectives for the central Arctic caribou herd and other wildlife populations have been met during the period of oil field development and operation. Although there may be some subtle impacts on individual animals, the herd, which is the unit of management, has grown. These points were emphasized in a paper published in the journal *Biological Conservation* but also ignored in the NRC report.

It must be acknowledged that the caribou herd that calves in ANWR (the Porcupine caribou herd) differs from the central Arctic herd near Prudhoe Bay in several ways. The Porcupine herd migrates over a larger range in Alaska and Canada. Calves are often born on the coastal plain of ANWR where the best oil prospects are thought to be. Caribou of the Porcupine herd can occur in groups numbering tens of thousands, much larger than the groups of hundreds to thousands in the central Arctic herd at Prudhoe Bay. These factors suggest that the Porcupine herd may be more vulnerable to disturbance and displacement than the central Arctic herd. However, depending on the year, calving occurs from the Yukon Territory, Canada, in the east, to the western edge of the refuge. There is potentially alternative calving habitat should parts of the ANWR be developed. In addition, caribou continue to calve in areas with oil fields, and avoidance of the roads and facilities is limited to a few weeks around the calving period.

Developing ANWR and Preserving Wildlife

I believe the experience at Prudhoe Bay indicates that we could achieve the multiple objectives of oil and gas development and maintenance of wildlife populations in the Arctic National Wildlife Refuge. The most obvious point is that impacts from oil development could be mitigated by some simple measures such as minimizing infrastructure and restricting industrial activity during the calving period.

However, we must give the public and elected representatives the truth about potential environmental impacts. This has not been happening because of biased reporting by biologists and environmental groups.

Clearly this is not unique to the ANWR issue. . . . Scientists and stakeholders in the resource industries must continue to aggressively present factual information, and correct biased reporting. It is apparent that different industries, including ranching, oil, mining, fishing, and timber, face the same bias in dealing with environmental issues. Perhaps increased communication and coordinated approaches among industry groups can help.

5

Developing the ANWR Is the Right of Alaskan Natives

Tara Sweeney

*Tara Sweeney, a native Inupiat Alaskan, has worked in govern-
ment relations for the Arctic Slope Regional Corporation (ASRC)
for more than a decade. The ASRC has sought to ensure that
profits derived from oil exploration and other resources benefit
the indigenous Inuit peoples. With the backing of this organization, Sweeney has lobbied the U.S. government to open the Arctic National Wildlife Refuge for oil drilling.*

*For the Inupiat people, the only indigenous people living within
the boundaries of the Arctic National Wildlife Reserve (ANWR),
opening the Coastal Plain for oil development offers numerous
benefits. The taxes and industry accompanying oil exploration
will lead to improved living standards, including indoor plumb-
ing, improved educational systems, and increased income from
higher-paying jobs. The drilling land within the ANWR was
given to the Inupiat peoples to control, and they have the right
to develop it as they see fit. Blocking oil exploration and drilling
within ANWR denies the Inupiat people the right to pursue a
better life and the opportunity to preserve their culture for future
generations.*

If you listened only to the news media and environmentalists, you'd think the debate over oil development in the Arctic National Wildlife Refuge (ANWR) was about caribou and
ecology. It's not.

ANWR is about land. It is about Alaskan Natives' rights of self-determination—our right to decide how our own lands and resources will be used. About whether the United States will honor its agreements with Natives who ceded their claim to vast ancestral lands and resources, in exchange for the right to determine our destiny on the lands we retained—or so we were told.

It's about whether senators, congressmen, pressure groups and other people who live hundreds or even thousands of miles from our lands will have the right to dictate our future.

Anyone who professes to respect Native rights, civil rights, human rights and property rights has only one choice in this matter. They must support what Native Americans who live in ANWR overwhelmingly want: drilling in accord with guidelines that we will negotiate ourselves.

Anything less is cultural and environmental imperialism. It is stealing our Native lands, resources and futures. It will keep our people on the edge of poverty forever. It is wrong.

The Need for Basic Amenities

Right now, it's 30 below zero in Kaktovik, the only village within the entire 19.6 million acres of the federally recognized boundaries of ANWR. It is total 24-hour darkness, and the wind is howling. Beyond the little houses, there is flat frozen ocean and tundra for as far as the eye can see. Stretching 1000 miles from the Barents Sea near Siberia in the west, to the Canadian border in the east, the Arctic Coastal Plain is one of the harshest climates in the world. Only the strongest people survive.

The Gwich'in have become the poster children of the anti-drilling movement.

The pure luxury of running water, flush toilets, local schools, local health care clinics, police and fire stations, were unavailable prior to the discovery of oil at Prudhoe Bay, America's largest oil field, 90 miles to the west. Kaktovik was the last community on Alaska's North Slope to get these wondrous things, courtesy of tax revenue from oil operations at Prudhoe Bay.

What would Americans in the Lower 48 States do if they were denied these basic necessities? They'd scream bloody murder!

Yet these are the basic amenities that radical environmentalists of the Sierra Club and Wilderness Society say the Inupiat Eskimo people should be denied. Some Gwich'in Indians in Alaska's interior agree. They can afford to. They are funded quite lavishly by green groups for opposing oil development on Inuit lands—even as they leased and drilled for oil on their own tribal lands, in the middle of caribou migration areas. But for opposing oil development on Inuit lands, the Gwich'in have become the poster children for the anti-drilling movement.

The Right to Control the Land

Even worse, many members of Congress also want to deny the Inupiat people of ANWR one of the most basic principles of our society: the right to own, control and use our private property.

My Inupiat Eskimo people are freezing in the dark, and with one breath members of Congress are preventing them from developing oil and gas on our own private lands in ANWR. With the next breath, they are pleading for gas and heating oil subsidies for their constituents. These actions are appalling and offensive to my people.

"The Inupiat Eskimo people are subsistence hunters," says Jacob Adams, president of the Arctic Slope Regional Corporation. "Based on close personal experience, we know we can have carefully regulated oil exploration and development in the Coastal Plain study area. We can preserve the environment and wildlife resources of ANWR—and still provide economic and energy security benefits to our people and the Nation."

Congress created and set aside the Coastal Plain specifically for oil and gas exploration—to compensate the Inuit for having given up rights to their other ancestral lands, and as a compromise for designating other Alaskan lands as wilderness. The 1.5-million-acre [reservation] is larger than Delaware, in a refuge the size of South Carolina. But Kaktovik's 92,000 acres of private land have been trapped, locked up and made untouchable by crass political forces, because it lies within the borders of ANWR.

Any oil or land development here can take place only with Congressional approval. The Native people of Kaktovik overwhelmingly support drilling. We know the tax revenues from oil exploration on our land will fund our basic utilities, educate our children, and preserve our culture and heritage.

But our rights and wishes are being trampled under foot—for no good reason.

The operations here are easily the most community involved, environmentally strict and technologically advanced anywhere in the world.

A History of Safety and Conservation

In 1970, when oil development was first proposed at Prudhoe Bay, my people in the Arctic Native community were understandably concerned and hesitant about our future and the effect of development on our homelands. Would the whales and caribou be chased away forever? Would our culture be destroyed?

To meet these concerns and challenges, and ensure the preservation of Native lands and heritage, Inupiat leaders, the Alaskan government, oil industry and federal government have managed a symbiotic, rational and successful relationship. Indeed, the operations here are easily the most community involved, environmentally strict and technologically advanced anywhere in the world.

The results are equally clear. During three decades of oil development, 3,000 caribou have turned into 32,000. Not a single species of animal, fish, bird or insect has declined even a fraction. Whales are harvested every year, as always. Neighboring Native communities have thrived, and cultures have been preserved and promoted. And many Native Alaskans have professional jobs in the oil industry.

Hypocrisy and Insult

Even the hypocritical Gwich'in—who want to stop all development in ANWR—operate Gwich'in Ensign Oilfield Services, Mackenzie Aboriginal Corporation, Mackenzie Valley Construction, Camp MGK, Gwich'in Helicopters and Inuvik Commercial Properties. Every one is directly involved in oil field services and contracts. They enable Gwich'in men and women to return to nice homes with decent paychecks and the satisfaction that comes from being involved in managing their own land for the benefit of their families and people.

That is why Kaktovik vice mayor the late Herman Aishanna said: "The strange people who want to call our country wilderness, to deny that we even exist—these people insult us. We know and understand the oil people, and we can handle them, as we have done for some years now." Former North Slope Borough mayor George Ahmaogak and the vast majority of all our people echo these sentiments.

Kaktovik wants its rights and wishes honored. This shameful, unconscionable treatment of Alaska's Native People—in the name of protecting lands that are in no danger—must end.

We urge all decent Americans to call their senators and congressmen, and tell them to vote for drilling in ANWR. The Natives who actually live there want this. Our nation needs it.

It will be good for the environment. And it will provide jobs, revenues and energy for Natives and non-Natives alike.

6

Alaskans Support Drilling in the ANWR

Kim Duke

Kim Duke is the former executive director of Arctic Power, an advocacy organization that works to persuade the U.S. government to open the Arctic National Wildlife Refuge for oil exploration and development.

The majority of funds in Alaska's state budget come from the oil and gas industry. As a result, many Alaskans see the economic benefit of allowing oil companies to begin drilling for oil in the Arctic National Wildlife Refuge (ANWR). The federal government must take these individuals' viewpoints into consideration when deciding whether to open ANWR for drilling because these are the individuals that have the most to gain or lose from development.

On April 10, [2003] the U.S. House of Representatives voted 228-197 to retain language opening the coastal plain of the Arctic National Wildlife Refuge (ANWR) to responsible oil and gas development (in H.R. 6, the Energy Policy Act of 2003). The vote margin of 31, which defeated an amendment by Congressman Edward Markey (D-Mass.) to strip ANWR language from the bill, nearly doubles that of an identical amendment Congressman Markey proposed to H.R. 4 in August 2001.

This strong message of support for development of the coastal plain of ANWR is extremely important as the cam-

Kim Duke, "Opening ANWR! As Arctic Power Lobbies to Open ANWR, Alaskans Get Closer to the Goal of Opening up the Coastal Plain to Oil and Gas Development," *Alaska Business Monthly*, vol. 19, June 2003, p. 22. Copyright © 2003 Kim Duke. Reproduced by permission.

paign continues in Congress. And yes, it will continue! Just as Mark Twain assured the public his demise had been greatly exaggerated, so are reports on the demise of legislation opening the coastal plain exaggerated. Anti-oil factions have made such proclamations many times before. However, Americans in general and Arctic Power in particular will not allow this area's world-class petroleum resources to be forever locked away.

Arctic Power's Role

Formed in 1992, Arctic Power is a nonprofit organization advocating jobs and energy for Americans through development of the resources of the coastal plain of ANWR. We seek congressional and presidential approval of legislation to allow responsible oil and gas exploration and production within ANWR's promising coastal plain.

A 52-member board of directors runs Arctic Power, a grassroots coalition of citizens from Alaska and across the nation who hail from a full economic spectrum. The board works closely with Alaska's U.S. congressional delegation, the Alaska State Legislature and Alaska's governor.

Arctic Power has generated a powerful coalition of support in Alaska and throughout the country. Local and national unions have joined Alaska Natives, business, trade and association leaders, all working together to educate Congress on the need for greater domestic production of oil and gas.

[Environmental] organizations profit at the expense of Alaskans, and indeed at the expense of all Americans.

This coalition has kept Arctic Power on the frontlines of the ANWR campaign, successfully assisting our delegation on more than 20 votes in Congress. We have realized remarkable successes in the campaign over the years, highlighted by legislation that passed the House and Senate in 1995—which was unfortunately then vetoed by President [Bill] Clinton.

Support for Development from Alaskans

Development of the coastal plain is now the centerpiece of President [George W.] Bush's energy plan and has been supported by leadership in the House and Senate. Even given this support, the campaign to open the coastal plain has suffered setbacks.

The setbacks were caused by green [environmental] organizations that have profiled enormously over the years through a massive disinformation campaign against the opening of the coastal plain. These organizations profit at the expense of Alaskans, and indeed at the expense of all Americans.

Alaska Has a Beneficial Relationship with Oil

Alaska's operating budget is more than 80 percent dependent on revenues from oil and gas production. Leasing alone could generate an estimated $2 billion in state and federal revenues within three years. Development of the coastal plain could generate 170,000 to 575,000 jobs nationwide and double Alaska's oil production to 2 million barrels per day, lessening our nation's dependence on foreign sources of oil.

Alaskans know from 25-plus years of experience in the Prudhoe Bay area [oil fields] that oil development's impact on wildlife and the environment can be mitigated. The Central Arctic herd [of caribou], which migrates through the area, has grown more than 8 percent a year with good calf production and survival, and high survival of adults. New technology has led to a dramatic reduction in the size of the footprint [surface area needed for oil production equipment and building of needed infrastructure] of oil development on the Slope.

Legislation moving through Congress requires use of the best available technology for development, and ensures that oil and gas exploration, development and production activities in the area will result in no significant adverse effect on fish and wildlife, their habitat and environment. Given that the Porcupine caribou herd often fails to reach the coastal plain to calve, and when it does, spends a maximum of six weeks a year in the area, it is clear that impact can be mitigated.

7

The Risk of Oil Spills Should Deter Drilling in the ANWR

Jason Leopold

Jason Leopold, author of the book News Junkie, *has more than a decade's worth of experience as a journalist for various publications. He has reported on issues such as the California energy crisis and the Enron scandal. Leopold currently contributes articles on U.S. government policy to liberal, online publications such as* Truthout, CounterPunch, Raw Story, *and* Z Magazine.

The prior conduct of oil companies operating in the Prudhoe Bay oil fields in Alaska has raised concern among individuals opposed to expanding domestic drilling operations to the Arctic National Wildlife Refuge (ANWR). Since 2001, numerous employees for British Petroleum (BP) have come forward alleging that the company does not always operate within its guidelines, and often fails to report oil spills and repair failing equipment. This irresponsibility suggests that these corporations are capable of acting in a manner that puts the environment at risk and may result in future oil spills in the ANWR if it were opened for development.

It's true that thousands of caribou and other types of wildlife will be displaced if Washington D.C. lawmakers pass a measure to allow drilling in the Arctic National Wildlife Refuge.

But there's an even bigger issue floating under the radar: the very real possibility of an environmental tragedy that

Jason Leopold, "It Could Be Worse Than the Exxon Valdez: Drilling and Spilling in ANWR," *CounterPunch*, April 21, 2005. Reproduced by permission of the author.

could be as catastrophic as the 1989 oil spill caused by the *Exxon Valdez* oil tanker if swift measures aren't taken to address severe safety and maintenance issues plaguing drilling operations in nearby Prudhoe Bay—North America's biggest oil field, 60 miles west of ANWR—and other areas on Alaska's North Slope.

That's just one of many alarming claims that employees working for BP, the parent of BP Exploration (Alaska) Inc., the Anchorage company that runs the 24-year-old Prudhoe Bay [oil operation] on behalf of Phillips Alaska Inc., Exxon-Mobil and other oil companies, have made over the years as a way of drawing attention to the dozens of oil spills—three of which occurred between March and April [2005] alone—that could boil over and happen at ANWR if BP continues to neglect safety issues and the area is opened up to further oil and gas exploration.

As President [George W.] Bush renews his calls for opening up ANWR to development, some of those very same BP employees are blowing the whistle on their company yet again and are turning to the one person who helped them expose oil companies' cover ups on Alaska's North Slope.

Watchdogs and Whistleblowers

Chuck Hamel, an Alexandria, Va., oil industry watchdog has been leading the fight for the past 15 years against corporations' (BP, Conoco Phillips and ExxonMobil) shoddy crude oil operations in Alaska. The safety and maintenance issues that Hamel and the BP whistleblowers brought to the attention of Congress and the public were supposed to be addressed by the oil company. Back in the 1980s, Hamel was the first person to expose weak pollution laws at the Valdez tanker port and electrical and maintenance problems with the trans-Alaska oil pipeline.

Hamel, who is protecting the identities of the current whistleblowers, says not only do oil spills continue on the

North Slope because BP neglects to address maintenance issues, but the oil behemoth's executives routinely lie to Alaskan state representatives and members of the United States Senate and Congress about the steps they're taking to correct the problems.

The company also denies its employees' claims of safety issues at its crude oil production facilities on the North Slope. Hamel, however, has got some damning evidence on BP: photographs showing oil wells spewing a brown substance known as drilling muds, which contain traces of crude oil, on two separate occasions. Hamel says he's determined to expose BP's shoddy operations and throw a wrench in President Bush's plans to open up ANWR to drilling.

"I am going to throw a hiccup into the ANWR legislation," Hamel said in an interview. "Until these oil companies clean up their act they can't drill in ANWR because they are spilling oil in the North Slope." If oil companies continue to fail to address safety problems at the North Slope "they'll have another *Exxon Valdez*" type of oil spill on their hands, Hamel said.

On April 15, [2005] Hamel sent a letter to [New Mexico] Senator Pete Domenici, chairman of the Senate energy and natural resources committee, saying there have been three spills between late March and early April [2005], at a time when BP and two of its drilling contractors are under investigation for charges of failing to report other oil spills in late 2004 and in January of [2005].

"You obviously are unaware of the cheating by some producers and drilling companies," Hamel said in the letter to Domenici, an arch-proponent of drilling in ANWR. "Your official Senate tour" of Alaska in March "was masked by the orchestrated 'dog and pony show' provided you at the new Alpine Field, away from the real world of the Slope's dangerously unregulated operations."

Domenici's office said the senator is reviewing Hamel's letter. In that letter, Hamel also claimed that whistleblowers had told of another cover-up, dating back to 2003, in which Pioneer Natural Resources and its drilling contractor, Nabors Alaska Drilling, allegedly disposed of more than 2,000 gallons of toxic drilling mud and fluids through the ice "to save the cost of proper disposal on shore."

Claims of Unreported Oil Spills

Hamel has had his share of detractors, notably BP and several Alaskan state officials, who said he's a conspiracy theorist, and the federal Environmental Protection Agency [EPA].

But Hamel was vindicated in March [2005], when Alaska's Department of Environmental Conservation confirmed Hamel's claims of major spills in December 2004 and July 2003 at the oil well owned by BP and operated by its drilling contractor, Nabors, on the North Slope, which the company never reported as required by state law.

The state of Alaska is in cahoots with the oil industry and routinely fails to enforce laws.

Hamel filed a formal complaint in January [2005], with the EPA, claiming he had pictures showing a gusher spewing a brown substance. An investigation by Alaska's Department of Environmental Conservation determined that as much as 294 gallons of drilling mud was spilled when gas was sucked into wells, causing sprays of drilling muds and oil that shot up as high as 85 feet into the air.

Because both spills exceeded 55 gallons, BP and Nabors were obligated under a 2003 compliance agreement that BP signed with Alaska to immediately report the spills. That didn't occur, said Leslie Pearson, the agency's spill prevention and emergency response manager.

BP spokesman Daren Beaudo said the company did report the spills after learning about it and said the spill wasn't that big of a deal.

"In this case, the drilling rig operators did not feel this type of event qualified for reporting," Beaudo told the *Anchorage Daily News* in March [2005]. "Obviously the Alaska Department of Environmental Conservation felt otherwise and that's what they're saying as a result of their investigation. It's a matter of interpretation." Beaudo said the agency's findings are in line with BP's own investigation that the spills did not cause any harm to the environment, aside from some speckles on the snow.

But what's troubling to Hamel is that Alaska's Department of Environmental Conservation has let BP off with a slap on the wrist. The agency is not penalizing BP; rather it said that it will ensure that the company reports other spills in a timely manner.

That plays into Hamel's other theory: that the state of Alaska is in cahoots with the oil industry and routinely fails to enforce laws that would hold those companies liable for violating environmental regulations.

A History of Neglect

In April of 2001, whistleblowers informed Hamel and Interior Secretary Gale Norton, who at the time was touring the Prudhoe Bay oil fields that the safety valves at Prudhoe Bay, which kick in in the event of a pipeline rupture, failed to close. Secondary valves that connect the oil platforms with processing plants also failed to close. And because the technology at Prudhoe Bay would be duplicated at ANWR that means that the potential for a massive explosion and huge spills are very real.

"A major spill or fire at one of our [processing centers] will exit the piping at high pressure, and leave a half-mile-wide oil slick on the white snow all the way," Hamel said at the time in an interview with the *Wall Street Journal*

That type of catastrophic scenario was wiped out of everyone's minds after 9/11 happened.

But then in March of 2002, a BP whistleblower brought up the very same issues and went public with his claims of maintenance backlogs and employee shortages at Prudhoe Bay that he said could worsen spills on the North Slope, particularly if ANWR is opened up to exploration.

The whistleblower, Robert Brian, who worked as an instrument technician at Prudhoe Bay for 22 years, had a lengthy meeting with aides to Senators Joseph Lieberman and Bob Graham, both Democrats, to discuss his claims.

At the time, Brian said he supported opening up ANWR to oil exploration but said BP has imperiled that goal because it is "putting Prudhoe workers and the environment at risk."

The Senate never held hearings on the safety issues that ... caused dozens of oil spills ... on the North Slope.

"We are trying to change that so we don't have a catastrophe that ends up on CNN and stops us from getting into ANWR," according to a March 13, 2002 report in the *Anchorage Daily News*.

In 2001, the Alaska Oil and Gas Conservation Commission found high failure rates on some Prudhoe wellhead safety valves. The company was put on federal criminal probation after one of its contractors dumped thousands of gallons of toxic material underground at BP's Endicott oil field in the 1990s. BP pleaded guilty to the charges in 2000 and paid a $6.5 million fine, and agreed to set up a nationwide environmental management program that has cost more than $20 million.

But Hamel and the whistleblowers, including Brian, said BP continued to violate environmental rules and then attempted to cover it up.

A BP spokesman said those claims "are an outright lie."

Government Remains Quiet and BP Does Not Clean Up

Still, despite the charges leveled against BP by the whistleblowers, which were aired as early as April 2001, the Senate never held hearings on the safety issues that over the years have caused dozens of oil spills at oil production facilities on the North Slope. Drilling in ANWR and President Bush's energy bill took a backseat following the 9/11 terrorist attacks and the ensuing war in Iraq. Now, with gasoline prices soaring and Bush's claims that drilling in ANWR would reduce this country's dependence on foreign oil, lawmakers are being urged to once again investigate the issue and hold hearings before approving any legislation that would open up ANWR to development.

BP has long been criticized for poorly managing the North Slope's aging pipelines, safety valves and other critical components of its oil production infrastructure. The company has in the past made minor improvements to its valves and fire detection systems and hired additional employees but has dropped the ball and neglected to maintain a level of safety at its facilities on the North Slope, Hamel said.

"Contrary to what President Bush has been saying, the current BP Prudhoe Bay operations—particularly the dysfunctional safety valves—are deeply flawed and place the environment, the safety of the operations staff and the integrity of the facility at risk."

8

The Lack of Viable Alternatives Should Encourage Drilling in the ANWR

Paul K. Driessen

Paul K. Driessen holds a bachelor of science degree in geology, a law degree from the University of Denver College of Law, and an accreditation in public relations. He has provided services to numerous conservative organizations on environmental topics such as global warming, oil drilling, and energy policy. He wrote the book Eco-Imperialism: Green Power, Black Death, *which criticizes the logic and tactics of the environmental movement.*

Whenever Congress proposes drilling in the Arctic National Wildlife Refuge (ANWR), environmentalists counter that the government and private industry should instead be pursuing alternative sources of energy that are eco-friendly. However, the methods of energy production they champion—such as wind power—are currently too impractical and inefficient to supply America's needs. Drilling for oil in the ANWR is a practical course of action that would result in minimal environmental destruction while boosting the nation's energy security.

The [2006] U.S. Senate budget bill would finally open the Arctic National Wildlife Refuge (ANWR) to drilling. Environmentalists are shocked and outraged. "This battle is far from over," they vowed.

Indeed, the 51–49 margin [of the Senate vote] underscores the ideological passion of drilling opponents, their party-line determination to block [George W.] Bush Administration initiatives, the misinformation that still surrounds this issue, and a monumental double standard for environmental protection.

Many votes against drilling came from California and Northeastern senators who have made a career of railing against high energy prices, unemployment and balance of trade deficits—while simultaneously opposing oil and natural gas development in Alaska, the Outer Continental Shelf, western states and any other areas where petroleum might actually be found. Drilling in other countries is OK in their book, as is buying crude from oil-rich dictators, sending American jobs and dollars overseas, reducing US royalty and tax revenues, imperiling industries that depend on petroleum, and destroying habitats to generate "ecologically friendly" wind power.

This political theater of the absurd is bad enough. But many union bosses also oppose drilling, and thus kill jobs for their members—the epitome of hypocrisy.

Government geologists say ANWR could hold up to 16 billion barrels of recoverable oil. That's 30 years' of imports from Saudi Arabia. Turned into gasoline, it would power California's vehicle fleet for 50 years, and hybrid and fuel cell cars would stretch the oil even further. ANWR's natural gas could fuel California's electrical generating plants for years.

At $50 a barrel, ANWR could save the US from having to import $800 billion worth of foreign oil, create up to 700,000 American jobs, and generate hundreds of billions in royalties and taxes.

Environmentalists Ignore the Facts

No matter, say environmentalists. They claim energy development would "irreparably destroy" the refuge. Caribou doodoo.

ANWR is the size of South Carolina: 19 million acres. Of this, only 2,000 acres along the "coastal plain" would actually be disturbed by drilling and development. That's 0.01%—one-twentieth of Washington, DC—20 of the buildings Boeing uses to manufacture its 747 jets!

Electricity from wind is hardly a substitute for petroleum.

The potentially oil-rich area is a flat, treeless stretch of tundra, 3,500 miles from DC and 50 miles from the beautiful mountains seen in all the misleading anti-drilling photos. During eight months of winter, when drilling would take place, virtually no wildlife are present. No wonder. Winter temperatures drop as low as minus 40 F. The tundra turns rock solid. Spit, and your saliva freezes before it hits the ground.

But the nasty conditions mean drilling can be done with ice airstrips, roads and platforms. Come spring, they'd all melt, leaving only puddles and little holes. The caribou would return—just as they have for years at the nearby Prudhoe Bay and Alpine oil fields—and do just what they always have: eat, hang out and make babies. In fact, Prudhoe's caribou herd has increased from 6,000 head in 1978 to 27,000 today. Arctic fox, geese, shore birds and other wildlife would also return, along with the Alaska state bird, *Mosquito giganteus*.

The Promotion of a Substandard Alternative

But the [environmentalist organizations] Wilderness Society, Sierra Club, Alaska Coalition, Defenders of Wildlife, and Natural Resources Defense Council still oppose ANWR development—even as they promote their favorite alternative to Arctic oil: wind energy. Electricity from wind is hardly a substitute for petroleum—especially for cars, trains, boats and planes. And swapping reliable, revenue-generating petroleum for intermittent, tax-subsidized wind power is a poor tradeoff.

On ecological grounds, wind power fails even more miserably.

A single 555-megawatt gas-fired power plant on 15 acres generates more electricity each year than do all 13,000 of California's wind turbines—which dominate 106,000 acres of once-scenic hill country. They kill some 10,000 eagles, hawks, other birds and bats every year.

On West Virginia's Backbone Mountain, 44 turbines killed numerous birds and 2,000 bats in 2003—and promoters want many more towers along this major migratory route over the Allegheny Front. Bat Conservation International and local politicians are livid.

In Wisconsin, anti-oil groups support building 133 gigantic Cuisinarts [food processors] on 32,000 acres (16 times the ANWR operations area) near Horicon Marsh. This magnificent wetland is home to millions of geese, ducks and other migratory birds, and just miles from an abandoned mine that houses 140,000 bats. At 390 feet in height, the turbines tower over the Statue of Liberty (305 feet), US capitol (287 feet) and Arctic oil production facilities (50 feet).

The hypocrisy of this ecological double standard is palpable.

All these turbines would produce about as much power as Fairfax County, Virginia gets from one facility that burns garbage to generate electricity. But they'd likely crank out an amazing amount of goose liver paté.

In Maryland's mountains, off the Cape Cod coast, amidst the tall grass prairie country of Kansas and elsewhere, the tradeoff is the same: thousands of flying mammals and tens of thousands of acres sacrificed to wind power, to "save" ANWR. Better yet, America could generate nearly 20% of its electricity from the wind, says the American Wind Energy Association, if it devoted just 1% of its land mass to these turbines. What's 1% of the USA, you ask. It's the state of Virginia: 23,000,000 acres.

The alternative to no wind energy and no Arctic oil is equally untenable: freeze jobless in the dark, or spend countless billions to import still more oil from the likes of Hugo Chavez [socialist president of Venezuela who is critical of the United States] and the mullahs [ruling Islamic clergy] of Iran.

The Hypocrisy of the Gwich'in

The hypocrisy of this ecological double standard is palpable. So union bosses, greens and liberal politicians bring up the Gwich'in Indians [indigenous to Alaska], who claim drilling would "threaten their traditional lifestyle."

Inuit Eskimos who live in ANWR support drilling by an 8:1 margin. They're tired of living in poverty and using 5-gallon pails for toilets—after having given up their land claims for oil rights that Congress has repeatedly denied them.

The Gwich'ins live 150–250 miles away—and their reservations about drilling aren't exactly carved in stone. Back in the 1980s, the Alaska Gwich'ins leased 1.8 million acres of their tribal lands for oil development. That's more land than has been proposed for exploration in ANWR. (No oil was found.)

A couple years ago, Canada's Gwich'ins announced plans to drill in their 1.4-million-acre land claims area. The proposed drill sites (and a potential pipeline route) are just east of a major migratory path, where caribou often birth their calves, before they arrive in ANWR.

Many therefore suspect that the Gwich'in's role as anti-oil poster children has a lot to do with the fact that they have received at least $630,000 from the Wilderness Society and a herd of liberal foundations. In exchange, they've placed full-page ads in major newspapers, appeared in television spots and testified on Capitol Hill in opposition to ANWR exploration—while pursuing their own drilling programs.

ANWR Development to Protect the Environment

Alternative energy technologies are certainly coming. Just ponder how we traveled, heated our homes, communicated and manufactured things 100 years ago—versus today. But the change won't happen overnight. Nor will it come via government mandates, or by throwing an anti-oil monkey wrench into our economy.

It shouldn't come at the expense of habitats, scenery and wildlife, either. Anyone who cares about these things should support automotive R&D [research and development]—and ANWR oil development.

9

The Oil Industry Is Unlikely to Use Clean Drilling Technology in the ANWR

Bryant Urstadt

Bryant Urstadt is a journalist who has covered numerous issues from global warming to sports in publications such as Rolling Stone, *the* New Yorker, ESPN Magazine, *and* Technology Review.

Since drilling began in the Prudhoe Bay oil field in the North Slope Borough of Alaska in the 1970s, the technology used in all stages of the oil extraction process has continually improved. Today, drilling can be far less harmful to the environment than it once was. Ice roads that melt every year can be used instead of building large, irremovable transportation infrastructures, and fewer above ground oil wells are needed because of the precision of exploratory equipment. Environmentalists, however, argue that these advances are still intrusive, but they also claim that oil companies have repeatedly demonstrated that they are unwilling to utilize these technologies unless compelled by the threat of legal or government action. Unfortunately, the government has lifted many regulations on drilling and its ecological impact, and until Congress adopts sterner measures, the oil companies are not likely to invest in these technologies or feel the need to put them into practice.

Bryant Urstadt, "Wild Profits: The Arctic Refuge May Soon Be in the Hands of Big Oil. Will It Drill Clean?" *Technology Review*, vol. 108, April 2005, pp. 74, 76–77. Copyright © 2005 by the Association of Alumni and Alumnae of MIT. Reproduced by permission.

Central to the case for allowing exploration and drilling in the Arctic National Wildlife Refuge (ANWR) is the argument that new technologies will allow industry to get the oil out with minimal damage to the landscape and the wildlife. It is likely that this line of reasoning will be unfurled once again . . . when Republican representatives and senators are expected to pick up their battering ram and renew the charge at the gates of what has become the prize possession of the environmental lobby. The last assault, in March 2003, lost in the Senate, with 52 senators voting to delete from a larger bill a provision that could have opened the refuge for drilling.

The Arctic National Wildlife Refuge is that 79,000-square-kilometer slice of pristine wilderness or barren wasteland, depending upon whom one asks, east of Prudhoe Bay on the North Slope, the largest operating oil field in North America. This is a frozen land so out of the way that it attracts a mere 2,500 tourists a year. By comparison, tiny Sachuest Point National Wildlife Refuge in Rhode Island sees upwards of 65,000. Most of those who do visit ANWR come in the summer and head not for the plain, where the oil is, but 25 to 80 kilometers inland, where the mountains and the grizzlies are.

Temperatures range from 4°C in the summer to well below -20°C every day during the winter, with nary a wink of sun in December. The section of the refuge under dispute comprises 6,000 square kilometers of the coastal plain, and its fate has awaited a decision by Congress since it was set aside for further study in 1980. It is likely to hold four to twelve billion barrels of recoverable oil, which, though it may not feed the engines of America for even a year, is still a considerable amount. As one government report puts it so well, "The refuge is an area rich in fauna, flora, and commercial oil potential."

Reports to Congress Document Clean Drilling Technology

Leading the charge again will be Senator Pete Domenici of New Mexico, chairman of the Senate Committee on Energy and Natural Resources, who intends to add revenue from drilling leases, perhaps in the neighborhood of a couple billion, to the 2006 budget resolution. Drilling in the refuge isn't really a budget issue, of course, but treating it as such prevents the possibility of a filibuster, to which budget resolutions are immune. If the resolution passes, leases would have to be granted, on the grounds that budget items must be reconciled with reality. Since the last elections [in 2004] thinned the ranks of senators opposed to drilling, many watchers expect such plans to move forward, despite what ought to be resistance from Democratic senators friendly to environmentalism, like Barbara Boxer of California and John Kerry of Massachusetts.

In 2001, as the debate about the refuge was making its near-yearly round through Washington and the media, members of Congress were provided with a report from the Congressional Research Service (CRS) that described the extraction technologies proposed for use in the refuge. The report, "Arctic Petroleum Development: Implications of Advances in Technology," is for the most part optimistic about the industry's ability to extract oil while minimizing environmental damage. It was prepared by Terry R. Twyman, a geologist and now a staff member of the American Petroleum Institute, which represents the interests of the oil and natural-gas industries.

The CRS describes itself as the "public-policy research arm" of Congress, charged with providing "nonpartisan, objective analysis and research on all legislative issues." With a budget of some $80 million, the CRS maintains a huge staff of analysts who produce reports on any topic that might be debated, ranging from problems facing mortgage funder Fannie Mae to homeland security. Its reports are available only to members of Congress but often make their way to the public anyway, usually through the offices of legislators who feel they stand to benefit from them. "Arctic Petroleum Development," for example, can be found on the website of the American Petroleum Institute (API).

[Depth-sounding] vehicles do not produce the portable earthquakes that have agitated the environmental lobby in the past, but they are still sizable rigs.

If Terry Twyman, having taken a job at the API, might be considered pro-oil, that does nothing to diminish the importance of the report, which more or less represents the industry's best case. A look at this case may help clarify the issues involved, for anyone who is following the debate or simply trying to understand what the refuge may look like to the visitor in 2015.

Less Intrusive Exploration

When a new oil field is opened, each phase of its development—exploration, drilling, and production—may damage the landscape, and in each of these phases, technological improvements promise to reduce or eliminate that damage.

More particularly, exploration, as it is currently conducted, consists of building a map of subsurface data and then drilling. Acquiring that data can be disruptive. The crews needed often number more than 100, and they move across the landscape in container trains pulled by bulldozers. Depth soundings are initiated by "vibroseis" vehicles, multiton articulated trucks lugging around vibrating plates. The plates generate low-frequency signals detectable by "geophones," microphones placed in a grid over several kilometers in rows as close together as a hundred meters. Sometimes known as "thumper trucks," these vibroseis vehicles do not produce the portable earthquakes that have agitated the environmental lobby in the past, but they are still sizable rigs that must cover kilometers of ground within a huge network of geophones, each of which must be laid by hand.

The damage caused by moving such equipment about can be minimized, Twyman argues, by exploring the refuge during the winter, when the terrain is frozen, and using Rolligons, vehicles with wide, balloon-style tires that would exert no more pressure on the tundra than a caribou hoof. (One industry photo even shows a Rolligon rolling over a smiling roughneck.) Coincident with the advent of the Rolligon has been the increasing use of ice roads on the North Slope. Ice roads are laid by Rolligons over the frozen tundra in mid-December and can support larger rigs pulling the mobile homes that house the crew. Drilling pads, too, can be built of ice. The oil industry contends that frozen roads and pads make the effects of exploration nearly invisible—all traces simply melt away—and believes that it can extend the drilling season further into spring by insulating the ice platforms.

Proponents also argue that the increasing accuracy of seismic data—which now yields 3-D rather than 2-D maps and can frequently be analyzed in real time by remote supercomputers—means that fewer soundings are necessary. The trade-off, however, is that although 3-D imaging reduces unnecessary drilling on what prove to be dry wells, it also requires the embedding of more microphones to obtain information in the first place. That, in turn, means more ground covered, with possibly harmful results. In any case, since the 1980s, advances in exploration technology have cut the number of wells needed to find oil in a field. This is good both for the oil industry's bottom line and for the environment.

No Substitute for Drilling

As the CRS report so baldly puts it, though, "there is no substitute, yet, for drilling," both for testing the hypotheses of computer modeling and for bringing oil to the surface. No substitute, but the number of wells needed to verify exploration and complete extraction can hypothetically be reduced yet further through a variety of drilling techniques, including directional, "designer," and multilateral drilling.

In directional drilling, extended-reach drills and bits angle out from a single platform to reach widely separated reservoirs of oil, covering a horizontal distance that can be two to five times the wells' vertical depth. In the North Sea, such wells have reached eight kilometers in length. Designer wells use bits that can make tight turns to avoid obstacles while drilling. Multilateral wells lead several horizontal branches off a single master well. With 3-D modeling, designer and multilateral wells can reach smaller and smaller pockets of oil. Drill bits have also improved. Made with diamonds, they have become harder, making drilling faster and allowing shorter times on site.

Drill holes, too, have gotten slimmer, which means fewer "cuttings"—the waste material that surfaces during drilling—and fewer personnel needed to handle the equipment and the waste. Some of the associated equipment can be transported by air, which lessens the need for new roads. A related advance is the development of coiled-tubing drilling, first used on the North Slope in 1991. Where traditional rigs might be 60 meters tall and use nine-meter-long sections of interlocking pipe, coiled-tube drilling employs flexible pipe that can be carried on a spool (sometimes brought in by air), which means holes drilled faster with less equipment and a smaller drilling platform.

Environmentalists continue to doubt that Arctic exploration can be conducted with anything like minimal impact.

Much is made of the "footprint" of an extraction operation—the area it takes up—and Twyman reports that, overall, that has been much reduced as well. Drilling, for instance, produces enormous volumes of by-products, including water, natural gas trapped with the oil, and the cuttings fed up to the surface by a boring bit. These materials were formerly dumped into reserve pits six meters deep and around 4,000 square meters in area. Cuttings and water can now be pumped back into the ground. Furthermore, the water can now be separated from the oil while still underground, which alleviates the need for surface separation facilities. The general effect, industry contends, is smaller facilities manned by fewer men.

A Track Record of Destruction

Of all these technical advances, the environmental lobby, as might be expected, is skeptical. The Wilderness Society, for one, has published a report questioning pretty much every industry assertion about new drilling technology.

Environmentalists continue to doubt that Arctic exploration can be conducted with anything like minimal impact. Rolligons, they contend, are unlikely to work in the hilly terrain that characterizes much of the coastal plain; their low-impact tires simply will not propel them up a grade. Even ice roads, certainly the most elegant of industry solutions to environmental problems, are called into question. Environmental advocates point out that water is a limited resource in the Arctic refuge and is not, in any case, located close to likely oil fields. They also like to mention that global warming has dramatically shortened the arctic ice season. The environmental lobby fully expects that, if drilling is approved, industry will sidestep the Rolligons when needed by applying for exemptions and roll in heavier equipment.

There is good reason to conclude that big oil probably could drill clean, but probably won't.

As for drilling, environmentalists point out that directional wells on the North Slope have averaged around one and a half kilometers in length, reaching a maximum of six kilometers in one instance, and that they in fact turned out to be so expensive that BP [British Petroleum] abandoned them entirely in 2000. Environmentalists also doubt claims that exploration can somehow be confined to winter, pointing out that oil companies have never ceased production in the summer on the North Slope.

In these and other arguments, however, one begins to sense that environmentalists are not so much addressing the technologies themselves as industry's willingness to employ them, an interpretation borne out by the title of the Wilderness Society's report on the subject, "Broken Promises." The bulk of most environmental presentations, in fact, concerns not possibilities or drawbacks inherent in an approach like directional drilling but rather industry's poor record in employing old and new technology alike, complete with the usual photos of production facilities belching black smoke, the sprawling infrastructure at Prudhoe Bay, and roads crisscrossing the tundra. Environmentalists fully expect more of the same in the refuge.

More to the point, as environmentalists see it, the argument is not about technology at all. Fancy wells are still wells, less intrusive exploration is still intrusive, and pipelines remain pipelines (as well as the subject of the most laughably devious language in recent House bills regarding the refuge, which would limit the footprint of any industry activity—including the 150-kilometer or longer pipeline—to eight square kilometers but interprets the pipeline's footprint as that of the thin piers on which it would rest). None of these innovations, environmentalists contend, is compatible with wilderness, and they will turn a refuge into an industrial corridor.

The Necessity of Government Regulation

It is not beyond the bounds of reason, however, to imagine that industry *could* drill with acceptably low impact. Man is an intelligent animal, after all, and ought to be able to remove oil from the ground without devastating the surrounding area. Less philosophically, the legal fines attached to environmental regulations are a mighty motivator. David Masiel, a former North Slope oilman, addressed this topic in a 2004 article in *Outside* magazine. He visited the North Slope and had conversations with drillers, executives, and enforcement officials. He found a new culture of cleanliness, mainly inspired by the threat of expensive lawsuits, to the point that drillers were actually baking gravel free of spilled oil. Writing for a magazine that has previously taken the administration to task for its environmental policies, Masiel concluded that drilling could be done in the Arctic with a tolerable level of damage—but only if clean drilling was legally enforced.

Secretary of the interior Gale Norton, in testimony before the House in 2003, emphasized that "the administration views tough regulation as an essential part of the ANWR proposal." But the administration has squandered its credibility there—something that may not have been apparent when Masiel took his trip in 2002—and has in fact been rolling back environmental regulations at a historically unprecedented rate. Areas designated as "roadless" in the Tongass National Forest in Alaska, for instance, are no longer roadless, and protections for wildlife across the United States have been greatly weakened, as bird watchers in New York recently discovered when a famous red-tailed hawk's nest was removed from a cornice by finicky apartment dwellers. Rules that have survived are simply not enforced: old cases have been dropped, and new ones are decreasingly pursued. It is only realistic to imagine that the same standards will be applied to the oil fields.

The technology for drilling with low impact may be available. Based on the administration's record of legislation and enforcement, however, it is unlikely that industry will be compelled to use it. Those technologies, such as coiled-tubing drilling, that have already proven themselves to be both environmentally *and* economically advantageous may be employed. Those that significantly increase the cost of drilling will be shoved aside unless the administration mandates their use, which it will not. Industry is not a moral being but an economic creature responding only to economic stimuli. As such, given the current balance of power in Washington, DC, there is good reason to conclude that big oil probably could drill clean, but probably won't.

10

Environmental Concerns Should Not Stop Drilling in the ANWR

Eric Daniels

Eric Daniels, a PhD in American History, is a research assistant professor at Clemson University's Institute for the Study of Capitalism. He contributed a chapter to the book The Abolition of Antitrust *and some entries in the* Oxford Companion to United States History.

Environmentalists who lobby to keep oil exploration and drilling teams out of the Arctic National Wildlife Reserve consistently call for the reduction of oil use because of dwindling supplies, but they are against any exploration within the United States for new reserves. These radicals are more interested in protecting Arctic wilderness and animals than in finding viable ways for humans to live comfortable lives. America should not be restrained from tapping its own energy sources by irrational arguments that place the supposed rights of animals over the rights of human beings.

The war on terrorism, with its potential effects on the supply of Mideast oil, has generated a pseudo-debate over America's energy policy. The only two sides we hear are the environmentalists, who exhort us to use less oil, and the timid supporters of the oil industry, who are conceding environmentalism's basic premise.

The National [*sic*] Resources Defense Council's Robert F. Kennedy Jr., for example, calls on Congress to "reduce our dependency (on foreign oil)" by raising fuel-efficiency standards. *New York Times* columnist Paul Krugman argues that now is the time "to prevent another dangerous surge in oil consumption."

The Union of Concerned Scientists insists that we "secure our energy future" by "reduc(ing) our reliance on imported and domestic oil."

The ostensible rationale for cutting energy consumption is that America is running out of oil. Environmentalists point to the 33 percent decline in domestic production of crude oil over the last 25 years as a sign of impending scarcity. Given the new potential disruptions in Mideast supplies, they say, the only solution is for Americans to sacrifice their standard of living and make do with less.

Stopping the Search for Oil

As irrational as that "solution" is, a close inspection of the facts reveals a far more insidious agenda. The environmentalists' actual premise is not that we are running out of oil, but that the oil companies should be stopped from finding it.

Consider the controversy over the Arctic National Wildlife Reserve [*sic*]. In 1998 the United States Geological Survey found the reserve's coastal plain region contains between 11.6 and 31.5 billion barrels of oil—potentially 10 percent of U.S. consumption for the next 30 years.But it's legally off-limits to drilling. Why?

America's vast Outer Continental Shelf contains approximately 46 billion barrels of oil, according to the Minerals Management Service. There too, environmental controls severely restrict access to the oil.

The voices alleging supply is running short are the same ones opposing new exploration and development. For 30 years, environmentalists have been sealing off millions of acres of oil-laden reserves, thereby creating the decreasing domestic supply. Again, why?

Their concern about problems like oil spills is just a facade. Environmentalists are resistant to any technological advances that minimize the possibility of such occurrences.

And they are utterly indifferent to all the hardships caused by the absence of petroleum products that would otherwise be available.

Placing Wilderness Rights Above Human Rights

What they really believe is that energy producing per se is undesirable, because it "violates" the earth's natural state. According to the Sierra Club, bringing technology to the Arctic National Wildlife Reserve would "destroy the wilderness even if (drilling) is carried on with immaculate care."

The Alaska Wilderness League declares that "drilling the wildest place in America is objectionable no matter how it's packaged." And Democratic Sen. Joseph Lieberman says reserve development "would cause irreversible damage to one of God's most awesome creations."

Human beings have rights; wildernesses do not.

What damage? The "damage" of reshaping nature to serve human needs?

The ruse, by now, should be clear. What threatens us is not any physical scarcity, but a politically created one. Environmentalists want us to produce and consume less energy, because they value untouched nature above human comfort. The declaration by the radical group Earth First that our "industrial culture must be dismantled," is a consistent application of environmentalist ideology.

Almost as bad, though, is the capitulation by the alleged defenders of energy development. The American Petroleum Institute, for instance, argues for the reserve's development with the appeasing claim [that] the wildlife there will remain unaffected. And congressional Republicans, instead of categorically upholding man's right to use nature to sustain his life, are quibbling with their opponents over whether the Arctic National Wildlife Reserve will yield 30 billion or 13 billion barrels of oil.

These "defenders" should be asserting that the production of even a single barrel of oil should not be stopped by a wish to preserve the caribou or the tundra. Human beings have rights; wildernesses do not. Laying pipelines along a frozen wasteland benefits man; keeping that wasteland "pristine" does not. Today, particularly as the architects of our foreign policy worry about reductions in the output of Persian Gulf oil, there is one obvious way to ensure abundant, reliable sources of energy; free the American producers from the shackles of environmentalism.

11

Drilling in the ANWR May Help America Adjust to Higher Oil Prices

Ronald Nelson

Ronald Nelson is a geologist who has worked extensively within the oil and gas industry, spending most of his career with Amoco (which is now BP Amoco). He is the author of the book Geologic Analysis of Naturally Fractured Reservoirs.

Oil prices are rising because the global supply of oil has reached its peak. As prices go higher, the American public will be forced to cut back on oil consumption and learn not to waste the reserves that exist. To delay the shock of living in a world of reduced oil consumption, the nation should consider opening the Arctic National Wildlife Refuge to drilling. Any oil extracted will buy America more time to embrace fuel efficient vehicles and alternative energy sources.

With [ever-rising] gasoline prices . . . perhaps the time has arrived to begin the process of exploring and, if successful, developing the petroleum resources in the Arctic National Wildlife Refuge (ANWR) of northeast Alaska.

This 19-million-acre reserve is home to caribou, musk ox, polar bears, white wolves and other rare wild life. It is also home to the village of Kaktovik, a permanent Eskimo settlement. There are also nomadic people who follow the annual migration of the caribou herds in the ANWR. Adjacent to

Ronald Nelson, "Is ANWR the Answer to Our Energy Riddle?" *Pipeline and Gas Journal*, vol. 232, 2005, pp. 45–46. Copyright © 2005 Oildom Publishing Co. of Texas. Reproduced by permission.

ANWR, immediately to the west, is the Prudhoe Bay oil field, the largest oil pool ever found in the U.S.

This field was discovered in 1968 and went into production in 1978. More than 80% of its 13 billion barrels of oil reserves have been produced. This field also contains 26 Tcf [trillion cubic feet] of natural gas reserves, which have been stored to provide maximum oil recovery. Studies are under way on how to bring this gas to markets in Alaska, Canada, and the upper Midwest of the U.S.

For about 25 years, Congress has debated and even voted in 1995 in favor of ending the moratorium on exploratory drilling in ANWR, but this measure was vetoed by President [Bill] Clinton. . . .

Exploring the Unknown Oil of ANWR

No one knows with any certainty the amount of undiscovered petroleum which may exist in ANWR, but if the Prudhoe Bay field is used as a template, the potential is enormous. Only drilling can prove up oil reserves. All other surveys, whether seismic, gravity, magnetic or induction, can only indicate attractive drilling locations for exploration and development wells.

Initial exploration tests can be drilled with slim hole technology by heli-drill rigs to minimize the need for environmental damage. Once an attractive oil accumulation is identified, multiple development wells can be directionally drilled from a single pad in order to minimize the footprint of drilling activity. The future oil produced can be pipelined over the Prudhoe Bay field for transmission in the Alaska pipeline to Anchorage where tankers can load and transport it to refineries in the U.S.

U.S. government policy in Iraq has resulted in less oil production from that nation than was being produced before the war. It has become evident that the older fields in Iraq will require immense investments to repair the damage of 15 years of war and neglect.

In Russia, President [Vladimir] Putin has sent a chilling message to American oilmen by confiscating the assets of [Russian oil company] Yukos to pay back taxes that were in dispute. Much of the oil production that the world relies upon comes from Saudi Arabia, Kuwait, Iran, and the United Arab Emirates (UAE), and it must be tankered through the Straits of Hormuz, a 13-mile-wide channel between the UAE and Iran. This is the jugular of the world oil supplies to Europe, Asia, and the U.S.

The U.S. can also rely on Venezuela for its heavy crude oil, suited to U.S. refineries near the Gulf of Mexico. But policy toward this important nation has not been conducive to U.S. interests. President [Hugo] Chavez has threatened to reduce oil exports to the U.S and increase them to China.

The world is approaching a crisis in oil supply that is far more urgent than many other issues.

Perhaps it is time to open at least a portion of ANWR to exploration in order to determine its potential. The Alaskan pipeline will have plenty of capacity for oil as long as it is maintained. That cannot be relied on indefinitely, however, because when Prudhoe Bay area fields are depleted, there will be no incentive to maintain the pipeline unless it is used for ANWR. If the U.S. can begin exploring ANWR [soon], it is likely to take [ten years] to begin commercial oil production. By then, the Alaskan pipeline could already be empty.

The Inevitable Price Increase

Most oil executives are in denial about the state of depletion of the world's proven oil reserves. They tend to believe that current oil prices are an anomaly resulting from oil traders bidding up the price because of a terrorism premium. But, there is now a growing realization that the world is approaching a crisis in oil supply that is far more urgent than many other issues.

The transportation system in the 21st century is solely dependent upon oil, not natural gas. Abundant natural gas may help avoid a crisis in electrical energy generation, but it will not replace gasoline, aviation fuel, bunker fuel for ships and diesel fuel for trains and trucks. These all require refined oil products.

Some say that high oil prices are due to a lack of new refineries in the U.S. That is not the reason, however, because the U.S. has imported refined products in increasing volumes for decades. The reason oil prices are so high is the perception that the era of cheap oil is coming to an end. In the future, motor fuels will increasingly be produced from tar sands, oil shales and other exotic sources that will make today's oil prices look like a bargain.

Fortunately, supply and demand for oil is now regulated by price, not OPEC [Organization of Petroleum Exporting Countries]. This should give comfort to oil executives who must make large investment decisions in ANWR if discoveries are made. We will not run out of oil—it will just get progressively more expensive. The public will be forced to reduce demand because they cannot afford to waste it.

Remember when people used to car-pool? Maybe it will become fashionable again. Developing ANWR might just buy enough time to replace large SUVs with hybrid gas-electric vehicles. A trend is already starting in that direction.

12

Drilling in the ANWR Should Be Reserved for a Time of National Emergency

Perry A. Fischer

After working for two different offshore oil drilling companies, Perry A. Fischer became editor for the monthly journal, World Oil, *which provides information to both producers and consumers of oil products. In* World Oil, *he publishes articles concerning the exploration and exploitation of oil sources.*

Because drilling for oil in environmentally sensitive areas is a politically divisive issue, there should be a bipartisan agreement in Congress that oil companies will not develop the Arctic National Wildlife Refuge (ANWR) until America has a critical need for any reserves found there. Until such time, oil companies should be allowed to make surveys and accurately assess the oil deposits in the region. Delaying drilling may allow the global oil supply situation—which has been disrupted by war in Iraq and the possibility that Venezuela will nationalize its oil industry—to return to normal, and it would make clear that the ANWR is a strategic reserve.

By the time that you read this, it might be moot in some sense, but I've been waiting for more than a year for the Arctic National Wildlife Refuge (ANWR) 1002 Area [the Coastal Plain area where there is thought to be oil] debate to resolve, and, unless several Democrats vote with Republicans

Perry A. Fischer, "Exploring the Environmental Wilderness," *World Oil*, vol. 224, April 2003, p. 17. Copyright © 2003 WorldOil.com Inc. All rights reserved. Reproduced by permission.

or the Republicans reverse the current defection within their own ranks, there is still no end in sight. This situation—developing environmentally sensitive areas—is not unique to the US: many importing countries find themselves confronted with similar dilemmas. So, here's my plan—unselfishly, if not immodestly, offered—on how to bring the two sides together. The following hard-to-argue-with points might find common ground.

Even Relatively Small Amounts of Oil Help

Strategic interests. This argument ought to be particularly timely, in light of the current situation in Iraq and Venezuela. The geopolitical imbalance created between nations able to export oil and those that must import will only grow worse. Every billion barrels that do not have to be imported helps to avert war, promote economies and preserve human life. Such reasoning should appeal to both sides.

> *If commercial [oil] discoveries are made [in the ANWR], they would not be produced except in times of national emergency.*

It's not worth the risk. We've all heard the argument that radical or poorly informed environmentalists like to point out: namely, that 4.3 BBO [billion barrels of oil] is "only" about 10 months of US consumption, so it's not worthwhile. Using this flawed logic, no oil wells would ever be drilled. Non-oilfield folks simply do not realize that it takes roughly 35,000 wells drilled a year and 530,000 producing wells just to keep US production on a slow decline. Neither are they aware that the average well produces just 11 barrels a day; or that a good discovery is a reservoir that equals just *one day's* worth of US production.

While it's not possible to say that exploration and production activity will have zero impact on animal life—we have not banished the blowout [an uncontrolled oil eruption]—it is clear that with enough attention to detail, new technology, and yes, even watchdogs, the impact on wildlife populations would be minimal, if at all.

Geologic assessments are valuable, necessary and dangerous studies that further (or diminish) exploration interest and help get the argument going. But because they are generally statistical and based on assumptions, they can, and often are, twisted by ideologues. The US Geological Survey (USGS) uses a statistical bracketing method in its analysis. This means that within the ANWR 1002 Area, there is a big chance that there is at least some technically recoverable oil (4.3 BBO), and a little chance that there is a huge amount of oil (11.8 BBO). The mean is 7.7 BBO.

The real risk in delaying production indefinitely is time.

The problem here is that this "statistical oil" is not real, although these numbers continue to be debated as if it were. Oil companies perform similar analyses every day. Explorationists pore over reams of data, leases are bought, millions of dollars are risked, and most of the time, they come up empty-handed.

ANWR Oil for Emergencies Only

The solution to ANWR is the drill bit, but with a twist. Rather than lease, drill and produce ANWR in the usual way, it could be agreed upon beforehand that if commercial discoveries are made, they would not be produced except in times of national emergency. The area could be much better appraised with 12–24 wildcats [blindly placed wells]. Seismic data, acoustic velocities, cores, petrophysical data and so on could all be gathered and made public. Complex lease agreements would be necessary, with the federal government providing substantial incentives in exchange for public disclosure of the data and indefinite delay of production. But the effort would be worthwhile, because only with the drill bit can a true appraisal be made. And who knows? There just might be a great deal less—or more—oil there than anyone imagined.

The real risk in delaying production indefinitely is time. Assuming that substantial reserves are found, even in an emergency situation, it would be at least a year before one of those P&A'd (suspended) wildcats could deliver early oil, and about 3–5 years for robust development. We've seen the supply status turn on a dime. The situation in Venezuela compounded by Iraq could remove all of the world's excess capacity; but within a few months, both situations could abate, returning the world to an excess capacity of 3–5 million bpd [barrels per day].

What's in a name? Apparently, everything. First, WR stands for Wildlife Refuge. Immediately to the west is found the National Petroleum Reserve-Alaska (NPR-A). As much as anything—plant and animal diversity, habitat, utility of the land, etc.—the name alone seems responsible for much of the politicizing. For example, NPR-A has lease sales and exploration activity (with reasonable success) and, except for the occasional obstructionist lawsuit, E&P [exploration and production] activity proceeds without much fanfare. Remarkably, USGS says both areas have comparable volumes of technically recoverable oil (although NPR-A is farther from infrastructure).

So here's my proposal. Remove the warm, fuzzy and pathetic names—Wildlife Refuge and 1002 Area, respectively—and call it something marketable. How about iSTAR, for in situ STrategic Alaskan Reserve? I can see the ads now: "iSTAR—support America's future *and* preserve the wilderness."

Of course, in a political world, this entire rational diatribe hinges on whether drilling in ANWR has something to do with oil.

13

Proponents and Opponents of Drilling Have Exaggerated Their Claims

Bryan Keefer

Bryan Keefer is one of the cofounders of spinsanity.org, *a Web site dedicated to providing accurate information about issues that are constantly being reframed and skewed ("spun") by politicians and the media. The Web site officially closed down in January 2005, but Keefer's continued monitoring of the media and politicians has resulted in his coauthoring the book* All the President's Spin: George W. Bush, the Media, and the Truth, *and serving as managing editor for* brijit.com, *a Web site summarizing and rating online articles.*

The debate over whether drilling in the Arctic National Wildlife Refuge (ANWR) should be allowed has been contentious. Politicians who support drilling have made outlandish and exaggerated claims about the amount of oil in the ANWR and the potential positive impact of this oil on national security and the economy. Likewise, those who oppose opening the refuge have made overstated claims about the ecological damage incurred by drilling and have focused attacks on supporters who have ties to the oil industry. As long as the tactics do not change, it is unlikely that anyone will take the time to consider whether drilling in the ANWR is sound national policy.

The proposal to allow oil exploration in the Arctic National Wildlife Refuge (ANWR) ... [has] brought out overheated rhetoric from public officials and pundits on both sides. [In congressional debates] each did their best to frame the issue advantageously: Opponents charged it was big oil vs. the environment, and supporters suggested it was volatile OPEC [Organization of Petroleum Exporting Countries] goons vs. national security and freedom.

Both sides have treated the facts in this debate cavalierly. As journalists Seth Borenstein and James Kuhnhenn point out, environmentalists have often overstated their claims about the potential damage to caribou herds, while some supporters of drilling have exaggerated the amount of oil in the refuge. When the proposal finally came under consideration in the Senate [in April 18, 2002] (the House approved the proposal [in] August [2001]), the spin reached a new level as each side tried to tie its viewpoint to everything from the war on terrorism to the [George W.] Bush administration's energy task force.

Challenging Opponents to Duels

Sen. Ted Stevens, R-Alaska, took on opponents of drilling with a rare attempt at direct intimidation on the Senate floor. Attacking the idea that the Wildlife Refuge is wilderness, he claimed ... that "anyone who comes to the floor and says this is wilderness is a liar—a liar. Anyone who tries to pretend that somehow or another we are violating the law is a liar. If it was back in the old days, I would challenge them to a duel."

Stevens continued: "This area, the ANWR Coastal Plain, is not wilderness" because "it is hell in the wintertime—60 below." As Stevens should know, however, temperature has nothing to do with the definition of wilderness. He's twisting the meaning of the term—normally, "a place without people"—to crudely reframe the debate using nothing more than bluster.

Other proponents of the drilling plan tried to link their side of the fight to the war on terrorism by intentionally blurring the timeline so that the oil exploration looked as though it could have an immediate impact. Most experts (including an [oil giant] Exxon executive who testified before Congress) calculate that it would take six to 10 years to develop ANWR's oil reserves. Yet Sen. Kay Bailey Hutchison, R-Tex., claimed on CNN's "Crossfire" that "the idea that we would sit here and let countries in the Middle East decide if our economy is going to be stable, if we are going to be able to prosecute this war on terrorism, is outrageous."

Sen. Frank Murkowski, R-Alaska, picked up the theme on the Senate floor, suggesting that "the risk [to our national security] is very real. The risk may go beyond the risk associated with just a political view of this issue. . . . I would like to think every member of this body values not only the president but his office to see what is in the best interest of our country, our nation and our national security." Both Murkowski and Hutchison are clearly attempting to associate the current war on terrorism with oil drilling in the ANWR. But while national security may be a valid concern several years down the line, to make the claim that oil from the refuge will have an immediate impact is disingenuous.

Oil Industry Puppets

Not to be outdone, opponents of drilling have indulged in cheap shots of their own. Paul Begala [then cohost of "Crossfire"] attacked drilling supporter Hutchison on "Crossfire" with the question, "It seems to me the only rationale for a party for drilling in Alaska but against fuel efficiency is that you are following what big oil wants, aren't you?" Sen. Richard Durbin, D-Ill., recycled the same theme: "[ANWR] is the centerpiece of their policy because the people who wrote the policy, the special interest groups that sat down and crafted the policy, have another agenda. It isn't energy security; it isn't energy independence. It is about profitability."

None of this deals with whether drilling in the ANWR is actually sound policy—support for drilling does not by itself invalidate Republican arguments about national security or energy independence. The opponents' argument is just a way of discrediting drilling by association. That tactic is used by drilling proponents, too. Stevens suggested that "a real problem is the people who really take advantage of the nation when we are evenly divided, the minority of the population—2 percent—which represents these radical environmentalists."

With the proposal off the table for the moment . . . the debate will perhaps simmer down enough to allow reasonable consideration of the issue. Then again, maybe we'll simply see another round of distorted facts and challenges to face off at 20 paces.

Organizations to Contact

The editors have compiled the following list of organizations concerned with the issues debated in this book. The descriptions are derived from materials provided by the organizations. All have publications or information available for interested readers. The list was compiled on the date of publication of the present volume; the information provided here may change. Be aware that many organizations take several weeks or longer to respond to inquiries, so allow as much time as possible.

Arctic Power
425 Eighth St. NW, Washington, DC   20004
(202) 248-4468 • fax: (202) 248-6123
e-mail: feedback@anwr.org
Web site: www.anwr.org

Arctic Power has been working since April 1992 to convince politicians in the federal government to approve drilling in the coastal plain of the Arctic National Wildlife Refuge (ANWR). Individuals from all walks of life and professions participate as members of this nonprofit organization, supporting its mission of education and outreach to promote reasonable and safe oil development within ANWR. Arctic Power has published extensive fact sheets reporting the need and benefits of drilling in the coastal plain as well as outlining the pro-drilling side of the ANWR debate.

Cato Institute
1000 Massachusetts Ave. NW, Washington, DC   20001-5403
(202) 842-0200 • fax: (202) 842-3490
Web site: www.cato.org

The Cato Institute, a libertarian public policy organization, researches and provides policy suggestions to the government, emphasizing the values of democracy, a free market economy, and limited government. Cato analysts insist that privatizing development of the ANWR oil reserves would provide the best opportunity to utilize this natural resource, and while ANWR oil might not increase national security or reduce U.S. energy problems, they argue that market-driven policies provide better solutions than political decisions. Cato fellows have authored reports such as "ANWR's Private Potential," "Energy Illogic," and "Don't Worry About Energy Security," providing information on these views.

City of Kaktovik
PO Box 27, Kaktovik, AK   99747
(907) 640-6313 • fax: (907) 640-6314
Web site: www.kaktovik.com

Kaktovik is the only city within the boundaries of the Arctic National Wildlife Refuge (ANWR). Native Inupiat people live in the city, which has been settled for centuries. The city of Kaktovik Web site provides detailed information from the Inupiat perspective on the land they inhabit, as well as their perspective on opening the coastal plain of ANWR for oil drilling.

Defenders of Wildlife
1130 Seventeenth St. NW, Washington, DC   20036
(800) 385-9712
e-mail: defenders@mail.defenders.org
Web site: www.defenders.org

From its founding in 1947, Defenders of Wildlife has worked to promote protection of wildlife and wildlife habitats worldwide. The organization's Web site *Help Save the Arctic National Wildlife Refuge* (www.savearcticrefuge.org) provides timely and compelling information detailing why drilling in the refuge should not be permitted. Additionally, publications on this site offer information about the impact of drilling on specific species such as polar bears, caribou, and birds; facts about the oil industry and oil supplies; and expert and public opinion on the issues involved.

Gwich'in Steering Committee

122 First Ave., Box 2, Fairbanks, AK 99701
(907) 458-8264 • fax: (907) 457-8265
e-mail: gwichinl@alaska.net
Web site: www.gwichinsteeringcommittee.org

Founded in 1988 to combat the increasing push from the U.S. federal government and industry to open the coastal plain in the Arctic National Wildlife Refuge (ANWR), the Gwich'in Steering Committee continues to promote preservation of the refuge in its natural state due to the land's cultural significance to the Gwich'in people. The committee published the report *A Moral Choice for the United States: The Human Rights Implications for the Gwich'in of Drilling in the Arctic National Wildlife Refuge*, detailing the importance of ANWR land and the wildlife that it supports.

The Heritage Foundation

214 Massachusetts Ave. NE, Washington, DC 20002-4999
(202) 546-4400 • fax: (202) 546-8328
e-mail: info@heritage.org
Web site: www.heritage.org

The Heritage Foundation is a conservative think tank providing information to the public and policy makers in support of conservative policies exemplifying ideals such as free enterprise, limited government, and a strong national defense. As a result, on the issues of drilling in the Arctic National Wildlife Refuge (ANWR), the foundation's stance is decidedly pro-drilling, based not only on arguments of free enterprise but also on the position that utilizing oil from ANWR would reduce America's dependence on foreign oil, thus increasing national security. Heritage reports detailing these arguments include "Opening ANWR: Long Overdue," "American-Made Energy from ANWR at a Modest Cost," and "Why Not Explore ANWR?"—all of which are available on the Heritage Foundation Web site.

Natural Resources Defense Council (NRDC)

40 West Twentieth St., New York, NY 10011
(212) 727-2700 • fax: (212) 727-1773
e-mail: nrdcinfo@nrdc.org
Web site: www.nrdc.org

The NRDC promotes international protection of wildlife and wild places through law, science, and a membership of over one million. Some of the main focuses of the organization include reduction of global temperatures, development of alternative technologies for energy, and protection of the world's oceans and endangered habitats. The NRDC has also focuses its attention on protecting the Arctic National Wildlife Refuge (ANWR) from being opened for oil development and drilling, publishing detailed reports such as "Arctic National Wildlife Refuge: Why Trash an American Treasure for a Tiny Percentage of Our Oil Needs?" and "Arctic Refuge 101: Fact Sheets," as well as a video outlining the negative impact of drilling in ANWR.

Sierra Club

85 Second St., 2nd Fl., San Francisco, CA 94105
(415) 977-5500 • fax: (415) 977-5799
e-mail: information@sierraclub.org
Web site: www.sierraclub.org

The Sierra Club, an environmental protection organization founded in 1892, works to ensure the conservation of natural habitats, preservation of species, and caretaking of the planet as a whole. The organization focuses much of its effort on combating global warming through innovative energy technologies and preserving American wilderness through public education and outreach. The Sierra Club also dedicates a section of its Web site to explaining the reasons why drilling in the Arctic National Wildlife Refuge (ANWR) should not be permitted and to providing opportunities for individuals to become involved in the campaign against opening the ANWR.

U.S. Department of the Interior (DOI)
1849 C St. NW, Washington, DC   20240
(202) 208-3100
e-mail: webteam@ios.doi.gov
Web site: www.doi.gov

The DOI is the U.S. government agency dedicated to protecting America's natural lands and resources and the accompanying recreational opportunities. Additionally, the organization works closely with native peoples across America to ensure their rights to the land are protected. DOI has been performing these duties since its creation in 1849. With regard to the Arctic National Wildlife Refuge (ANWR), the agency's position under the George W. Bush administration has been to promote responsible, environmentally sound drilling and development in order to fully utilize the natural oil reserves present in the coastal plain area. DOI has published fact sheets and reports detailing the impact of drilling in ANWR as well as the positive effects on the economy and national security.

Bibliography

Books

Subhankar
Banerjee

Arctic National Wildlife Refuge: Seasons of Life and Land. Seattle: Mountaineers, 2003.

Rick Bass

Caribou Rising: Defending the Porcupine Herd, Gwich'in Culture, and the Arctic National Wildlife Refuge. San Francisco: Sierra Club, 2004.

Matthew T.
Cogwell

Arctic National Wildlife Refuge. New York: Nova Science, 2002.

Kenneth S.
Deffeyes

Beyond Oil: The View from Hubbert's Peak. New York: Hill and Wang, 2005.

David Goodstein

Out of Gas: The End of the Age of Oil. New York: Norton, 2005.

Karsten Heuer

Being Caribou: Five Months on Foot with an Arctic Herd. Seattle: Mountaineers, 2005.

Roger Kaye

Last Great Wilderness: The Campaign to Establish the Arctic National Wildlife Refuge. Fairbanks: University of Alaska Press, 2006.

Chad Kister

Arctic Quest: Odyssey Through a Threatened Wilderness. Monroe, ME: Common Courage, 2003.

Michael T. Klare	*Blood and Oil: The Dangers and Consequences of America's Growing Dependency on Imported Petroleum.* New York: Metropolitan, 2004.
Hank Lentfer and Carolyn Servid, eds.	*Arctic Refuge: A Circle of Testimony.* Minneapolis: Milkweed, 2001.
Tom Mast	*Over a Barrel: A Simple Guide to the Oil Shortage.* Austin, TX: Hayden, 2005.
Debbie S. Miller	*Midnight Wilderness: Journeys in Alaska's Arctic National Wildlife Refuge.* Portland: Alaska Northwest, 2000.
Paul Roberts	*The End of Oil: On the Edge of a Perilous New World.* New York: Mariner, 2005.
Peter Tertzakian	*A Thousand Barrels a Second: The Coming Oil Break Point and the Challenges Facing an Energy Dependent World.* New York: McGraw Hill, 2007.
Jonathan Waterman	*Where Mountains Are Nameless: Passion and Politics in the Arctic National Wildlife Refuge.* New York: Norton, 2005.

Periodicals

Hal Bernton	"Alaska Native Corporation a Lead Player for Oil on Wildlife Refuge," *Seattle Times*, April 12, 2005.

Birder's World   "New Research Reveals International Importance of Disputed Alaskan Area," August 2007.

Joel K. Bourne Jr.   "Fall of the Wild: Our Appetite for Oil Threatens to Devour Alaska North Slope," *National Geographic*, May 2006.

Maria Cantwell   "Tap Our Minds, Instead," *USA Today*, December 21, 2005.

Zachary Coile   "Arctic Oil: How Much Oil Is Anybody's Guess," *San Francisco Chronicle*, August 30, 2005.

Ben Evans   "ANWR Still Divides Lawmakers," *CQ Weekly*, March 20, 2006.

Darren Goode   "Senators Say BP's Alaska Problems Doom ANWR Chances," *Congress Daily*, September 12, 2006.

Jennifer Hattam   "Slippery Slope," *Sierra*, May-June 2005.

Karsten Heuer   "Being Caribou," *Canadian Geographic*, March-April 2006.

Mac Johnson   "Prudhoe Bay Shutdown Involves Less than Half of Likely ANWR Reserves," *Human Events*, August 14, 2006.

Elizabeth Kolbert   "Wasted Energy," *New Yorker*, April 18, 2005.

Margaret Kriz   "Posting a Stop Sign," *National Journal*, September 9, 2006.

Peter Matthiessen "Inside the Endangered Arctic Refuge," *New York Review of Books*, October 19, 2006.

Susan McGrath "The Last Great Wilderness," *Audubon*, October 2001.

Todd Neale "Drive a Hybrid, Save the Arctic," *Audubon*, March-April 2006.

New York Times "Nature at Bay," May 9, 2005.

Sheryl Gay Stolberg "A Senator's Bold Ploy on Arctic Drilling," *New York Times*, December 21, 2005.

Robert Thompson "The Five-Minute Guide: Oil," *Esquire*, October 2005.

Nathan Thornburgh and Wesley Loy "A Crude Warning," *Time*, March 27, 2006.

USA Today "Arctic Drilling Makes Sense, but Don't Expect Miracles," March 23, 2005.

Scott Wallace "ANWR: The Great Divide," *Smithsonian*, October 2005.

Wall Street Journal "The Prudhoe Principle," August 8, 2006.

Mortimer B. Zuckerman "Our Energy Conundrum," *U.S. News & World Report*, April 25, 2005.

Index